PRAISE FOR NO YOUTH SOULUTIONS

Underneath his brilliant musical and ministry methods are humility, a vibrant faith, and a peerless character. God has used Alphaeus in a mighty way to affect the lives of thousands of students. I urge you to study his methods and walk in his instructions. You will be glad you did.

Lee McDerment
Anderson SC

The Stellar Award-winning Alphaeus Anderson is a hard-working, anointed young man with a humble, practical, and impactful gift dedicated to reaching out to youth with gospel music workshops. We have seen young people going from almost a whisper to melodiously bellowing out songs for Christ. There is a blessing in witnessing the hand of God working through him. We consider ourselves fortunate when we can get on his calendar at least once or twice each year.

Reverend Dr. Lonnie and Virginia Rector
Pilgrim Baptist Church
Newark, DE

It starts with someone like Alphaeus leading your middle and high school ministry. Alphaeus is leading a Stellar Award-winning youth choir. He is challenging the status quo and creating a model for how youth music ministry should look in our churches.

Pastor Travis Greene
Columbia, SC

Alphaeus and his wife have put together training modules and a plan to help our young people develop spiritually and musically. *No Youth No Church SOULutions* is the resource for those of us who continue looking for new ways to reach our youth, especially those in our churches. I tip my hat to Alphaeus for his steadfast work and for caring enough to put this book together. His integrity and consistency speak volumes.

Phillip Carter
White Plains, MD

Alphaeus and Alexias are anointed to do what they do. That's the only way to explain it.

Lejuene Thompson
Charlotte, NC

No Youth No Church SOULutions

The Power of the Missing Piece to Build a
Thriving Youth Ministry

Alphaeus Anderson and Alexias Anderson

JT PUBLISHING HOUSE
AL and Lex

No Youth, No Church SOULutions
Copyright © 2024 by Alpheaus Anderson and Alexias Anderson

Names: Anderson, Alpheaus. Anderson, Alexias.
Title: No/ Alpheaus Anderson and Alexias Anderson.
Summary: "Preserve your future with *No Youth No Church SOULutions: The Missing Pieces to Build a Thriving Youth Ministry*. This practical guide provides actionable strategies that you can implement right away to transform your church, whether it's small or large, into a vibrant community where youth and faith grow."-- Provided by author.

Identifiers: ISBN 978-0-9987587-3-2 (paperback) | ISBN 978-0-9987587-4-9 (ebook)
Subjects: BISAC: Religion /Self-Help/ General

All rights reserved. No part of this publication may be reproduced, stored in a retrieval system, or transmitted in any form or by any means--electronic, mechanical, photocopying, recording, or any other--except for brief quotations in printed reviews, without the prior permission of the publisher, as permitted under Section 107 or 108 of the 1976 United States Copyright Act, without either the prior written permission of the author or authorization through payment of the appropriate per-copy fee to the Copyright Clearance Center, Inc. 222 Rosewood Drive, Danvers, MA 01923, 978-750-8400, fax 978-646-8600, or on the web at www.copyright.com.

Scriptures taken from the Holy Bible, New International Version®, NIV®. Copyright © 1973, 1978, 1984, 2011 by Biblica, Inc.™ Used by permission of Zondervan. All rights reserved worldwide. www.zondervan.com The "NIV" and "New International Version" are trademarks registered in the United States Patent and Trademark Office by Biblica, Inc.™

Scripture taken from the New King James Version®. Copyright © 1982 by Thomas

Nelson. Used by permission. All rights reserved.

Scripture quotations marked (AMP) are taken from the Amplified Bible, Copyright © 2015 by The Lockman Foundation. Used by permission.

Scripture quotations marked MSG are taken from The Message, copyright © 1993, 2002, 2018 by Eugene H. Peterson. Used by permission of NavPress. All rights reserved. Represented by Tyndale House Publishers.

Scripture taken from the New King James Version®. Copyright © 1982 by Thomas Nelson. Used by permission. All rights reserved.

The Holy Bible, English Standard Version® (ESV®)

© 2001 by Crossway, a publishing ministry of Good News Publishers.

All rights reserved.

Disclaimer: Any internet addresses (websites, blogs, etc.) and telephone numbers in this book are offered as a resource. They are not intended in any way to be or imply an endorsement by the author, nor does the author vouch for the content of these sites and numbers for the life of this book.

Published by JT Publishing, Spartanburg, South Carolina
www.jtpublishinghouse.com

Printed in the United States of America
10 9 8 7 6 5 4 3 2 1

DEDICATION

We often say that if everyone in the world disappeared and we were left alone on this earth, our lives would feel devoid of purpose. But God, in His infinite wisdom, blessed us with the incredible gift of you—the students who light up our lives with your curiosity, passion, and unwavering faith. You are the reason we rise each day with a renewed sense of mission and strive to grow, learn, and give our best.

The Bible teaches us in Proverbs 22:6, "Train up a child in the way he should go, and when he is old he will not depart from it." This scripture is a powerful reminder of our responsibility to guide and nurture the next generation in the ways of the Lord. We believe that we are part of the village entrusted with this sacred task, helping to shape young hearts and minds to follow God's path.

This book is dedicated to you, the students who remind us daily of why God placed us on this earth. Your presence confirms our purpose, and we are honored to be part of the village that trains, guides, and preserves the things of God in your lives. Together, we are committed to instilling the values and principles that will anchor your faith, equipping you to stand firm in a world that often challenges what is good and true.

TABLE OF CONTENTS

Foreword..9

Chapter 1: Don't Read This Book......................................11

Chapter 2: The Journey..19

Chapter 3: Clarion Call..23

Chapter 4: Construction..31

Chapter 5: Calculated...43

Chapter 6: Captain..63

Chapter 7: Crew..75

Chapter 8: Creativity...95

Chapter 9: Community and Collaboration......................135

Chapter 10: Contend in the Culture..............................151

Conclusion..179

Acknowledgements..181

Meet Al and Lex...183

FOREWORD

It is a prized privilege for me to contribute an acknowledgement of the exceptional ministry of Alphaeus Anderson. Our connection has existed for years, but a recent incident illustrates why I regard the Andersons so highly. Alphaeus was already scheduled for our CCFM Conference 2024, to present to the general assemblage and to minister to a specific segment of our young people.

The day before the Conference began, we learned that a fellow youth instructor had to cancel at the last minute due to a critical family emergency. This matter left a serious void in the planned activities. We asked Alphaeus for a reference who might replace the original presenter. Without hesitation, Alphaeus volunteered himself (and his wife, of course) for those additional responsibilities, and—in addition to his original obligations—all bases were covered. This willingness to "go to the extreme" is a testament to his servant's heart and his passion that no young person goes untouched. I was deeply touched by such commitment.

God has granted Alphaeus, alongside his wife Alexias, the privilege of ministering to literally thousands of children and teens. This is not an exaggeration—it is a truth that attests to their profound calling and the precious anointing upon their lives. The fruit of their ministry is evident, as they have touched and impacted countless young souls.

In light of the Andersons' work, I cannot help but reflect on the current condition of many of our churches. Far too often, we fail to recognize the urgency of the hour regarding generational dynamics.

As a Pastor, I am typically positioned in front of a congregation during worship. However, on a few recent occasions, I have had that rare opportunity to sit behind various congregations: and I have noticed a concerning trend —most of the heads in front of me are consistently gray or white (or bald, like mine). This scene portends that these generations of faithful saints, as beloved as they are, will not be with us forever. At present, the quantity of the elderly vastly outweighs the number of youth in our churches.

The youth who should be filling our pews, first to positively and eternally shape their lives and then consequently to keep our ministries alive, are missing. Without their presence and engagement, our local churches are at risk of slowly fading away. If we do not intentionally raise the next generation in Christ, our ministries will dissolve into history.

Jesus declared, "Upon this Rock, I will build My Church, and the gates of hell shall not prevail against It." Notice He said His Church — not necessarily our churches. We must be careful not to conflate the two: His Church cannot fail, but our churches can. And they will if they do not prioritize the deliberate discipleship and preparation of future generations. All over the nation, numerous churches have already closed, and the reality is that, without strategic action, more will follow.

Hence, why Alphaeus' ministry is so crucial. We need his insights and the strategies he and Alexias have developed to disciple and train the next generation. Whether through children's Sunday school, youth groups, Vacation Bible School, or children's choirs, we must be purposeful in reaching our young people.

My desire for all local churches, networks, and denominations is that we will be committed to developing young Christ-followers on purpose. This work must not be a passing trend or a short-term focus but a long-term dedication to raising those who will carry the mantle of faith for future generations. Our efforts must be focused on building a sustainable, lasting impact.

Our recent Conference theme, "Next is Now," speaks directly to this need. If we neglect to invest in the next generation, our now will inevitably grow increasingly darker. But there is hope. There is a promise. By God's grace, we can impact the culture and move the younger demographics toward the light of the Gospel. Alphaeus and Alexias Anderson of Greenville, South Carolina, are key leaders in building momentum for this illuminating movement.

I encourage all who read this volume to engage in its message and mission fully. The future of our nations and communities, including our families and churches, depends upon it.

In The Service of the King,
Michael A. Blue

1
DON'T READ THIS BOOK

You are at risk of doubling your youth ministry in 6 months or less. Once the fire starts, fanning the flames is equivalent to the intentional laser-focused WORK you put into this area. Youth ministry takes work. The bottom line of the W.O.R.K. acronym is to think and open your mouth more.

What do I mean by that?

First, consider filling in the blanks below to help the acronym stick:

1. W_____

2. O_____

3. R_____

4. K_____

Answer Key:

1. Willing

2. Offering

3. Ready

4. Keys & Knowledge

Next, take a few minutes to write out what you want to see transformed in your youth ministry this year or the upcoming year. Take a moment to write down the plan your youth ministry will W.O.R.K. on for the upcoming year or the rest of the year.

Ephesians 3:20 always hypes us up in church. Imagine a Hammond organ starting when reading this scripture: "Now to him who is able to do exceedingly abundantly above all we ask or think, according to the power that works within us."

Did you feel that?

Did you feel work brewing?

That's what God is going to exceed.

We often hear, "Closed mouths don't get fed."

If you don't ask, there won't be any exceeding. If you don't strategize, think, or imagine anything, what does God have to exceed? It's like asking a teacher to grade a blank paper. Closed mouths and mindless behavior get subpar to zero results.

Which youth ministry will God likely do "exceedingly abundantly?"

Don't Read This Book

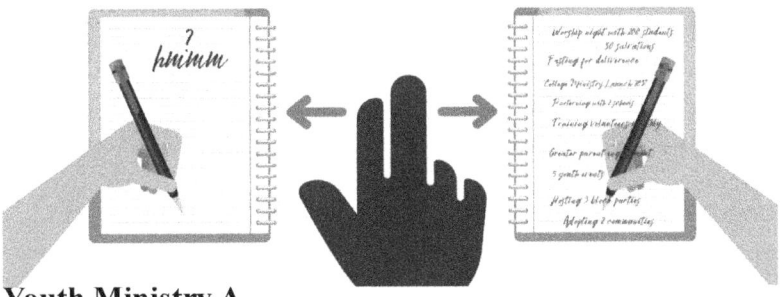

Youth Ministry A

We believe for a 200-member youth ministry

1. Provision
2. 50 salvations
3. College Ministry
4. Better volunteers
5. Partnership with two schools
6. Greater parent engagement
7. Five youth events

Youth Ministry B

Blank page

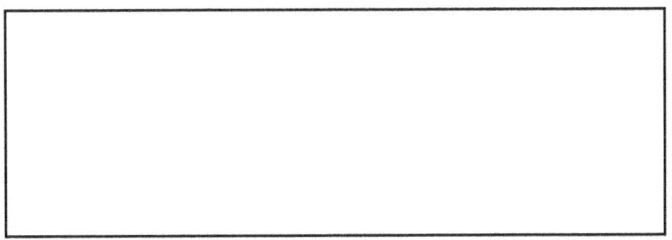

Listen, if you're not putting in the work, you can't expect any results. Straight-up hard work is the foundation of success in youth ministry. As Thomas Edison said, "Genius is one percent inspiration and ninety-nine percent perspiration."

You have to put in the effort to see the rewards. It's about dedication and commitment. There are no shortcuts or no easy ways out. The energy you invest is what you'll get back.

This book offers plug-and-play opportunities that can yield quick results, but remember, there must still be effort. Stay focused, grind, and believe your hard work will pay off. Success comes to the youth ministry that earns it.

Don't read this book if you are unwilling to put in the W.O.R.K. This book is the cheat-code that shows you how to roll up your sleeves and put in the W.O.R.K.

I often say if you ignore youth, they will ignore you. I understand youth ministry takes a lot of energy, sacrifice, resources, and man-hours, but increasing your numbers in youth ministry is one step away. Check the dirt on your shoes. More than likely, if a church has clean sneakers, they don't have a thriving youth ministry. There is no hack for man-hours. You get out of it what you put into it. If you decide to turn to the next chapter, your youth ministry is at risk of exploding in 6 months or less if you put in the work.

Imagine a single drop of water falling onto a rock. At first glance, it seems inconsequential, but that persistent drop can create a groove in the rock over time. This phenomenon occurs because of the consistent application of pressure over an extended period. The water's persistence and time wear down the rock, demonstrating how small, consistent actions can lead to significant changes.

John Maxwell's Law of Five states, "If you do the right thing every day in the right way, you will eventually achieve your goal." This law perfectly encapsulates the essence of persistent effort. Just as the drip of water relentlessly carves its path through rock, continuous focused effort in youth ministry will lead to impactful results.

Here's the encouraging part: while steady effort is crucial, you'll also be pleasantly surprised by some quick results. This book includes plug-and-play opportunities that offer quick wins, allowing you to see immediate progress. These quick wins can be incredibly motivating and show that your efforts are making a difference.

However, it's essential to remember that while you can skip steps for quick results, the foundation of your work is just as important. Consistent daily dedication builds the lasting impact you aim for.

AS YOU READ

"I and we" will be used interchangeably. Alexias and I (Alphaeus) are excited to combine our insights and expertise. Yes, my wife is smarter than me, so when you read the book and it sounds like a really good concept, it's probably me (Alphaeus) who wrote it (lol). We have been married for 18 years and jokingly say we are starting to look alike at this stage (haha). Seriously, when Alexias and I tag team, something magical always happens. It's like two ice cream flavors put together to make a new flavor.

What we have put together is not just a great book to read but a roadmap to help you discover your genius and become the top youth ministry in your city.

Therefore, we want to highlight a few things to increase your engagement with the book:

As you encounter phrases or thoughts expressed with bold bullet points or headers, we encourage you to give those points careful attention.

Throughout the book, we choose to use the word "situation." In each instance, please note that "situation" represents any entity in which students gather (e.g., church youth groups, youth ministries, and mentorship programs).

This book can be used as a workbook. It is important to us that you gain valuable insight as you read. Therefore, when asked to reflect, record your thoughts or fill in the blank, if provided. Take advantage of those opportunities. The spaces provided are a way to help you reflect on your experiences and make connections to your context.

1. There are moments to engage. We recommend participating and doing the activities.

2. Throughout this book, we'll discuss laying a strong foundation and ensuring that your youth ministry not only experiences quick successes but also achieves long-term transformation.

3. Finally, as you read stories or experiences that impact you, we encourage you to post those messages, insights, and revelations using #noyouthnochurch or #noyouthnochurchsolutions. You can also use a journal to capture your thoughts. Using a journal or sharing the connections you are making to the information often allows the importance of the topic to stay with you longer.

Stay consistent, stay committed, and keep building the foundation. Your steady efforts, combined with the strategies in this book, will yield significant, lasting results. A businessman said, "It's not about the 100th step; it's about the next step."

In other words, trust the process and take it one day at a time, and you will be well on your way to preserving the legacy of your local assembly.

NO YOUTH, NO CHURCH SOULUTIONS

2
THE JOURNEY

In 2003, amidst the changing landscape of hip-hop and the emergence of basketball sensation LeBron James, I, at 21, embarked on a mission to empower youth through a choir called Pure-N-Heart (PNH). Despite my lack of experience leading my "own" choir and the sparse attendance at our initial rehearsal, one child, Absalon, showed up, sparking a journey that would redefine my vision.

Though disappointed by the low turnout, Absalon's presence ignited a spark within me. Despite being prepared for a crowd, I taught him only one song. However, this setback didn't deter me. Over the next month, through perseverance and determination, our choir grew from one child to 125 active members from multiple states.

What began as a humble choir evolved into a movement, attracting youth far and wide. This accidental discovery of a youth-generating process transformed Pure-N-Heart into more than just a choir—it became a youth movement.

My wife, Alexias (not yet my wife), stood by my side, supporting the endeavor and helping check kids in at the Pure-N-Heart rehearsal. Her presence added an extra layer of encouragement and dedication to our cause.

Yes, it was hard leading a group of 100% volunteers to help manage a choir that grew to over 400 students. Think about it. Hundreds of churches in America are not even 400 members in size. We found ourselves in a situation where our vision was growing like wildfire. Students skipped soccer, cheer, and basketball practice to attend our rehearsals and workshops. The demand for more of what was usually a choir activity during the summer became great. Choir concerts turned into youth events, worship nights, empowerment sessions, national travel, and smaller cohorts, not to mention the curiosities from churches that asked, "How are you all doing what you are doing?"

Today, armed with this proven process, we continue to organize successful youth events, eager to share our journey and the results achieved through the eight areas this book will cover.

Here's a list of the areas to whet your appetite: Clarion Call, Construction, Calculated Consistency, Captain, Crew, Creativity, Community, Collaboration, Contend in the Culture.

HEAR OUR HEARTS

We are passionate about helping you transform your situation. Please do not mistake our passion for arrogance. We have seen youth ministries in our city experience a major decline, all while our efforts in youth ministry are flourishing. You deserve to flourish. Your youth deserve the best. Your youth deserve an energetic ministry experience and the opportunity to benefit from the life-changing impact. Allow us to help.

The principles in this book can be applied to areas beyond youth ministry. If you are reading this book and are not directly involved with youth ministry, our goal is to help you understand how impactful these principles can be.

NO YOUTH, NO CHURCH SOULUTIONS

3
CLARION CALL

A biblical clarion call is a clear and powerful command or appeal for action, often carrying a sense of urgency and importance. The term "clarion" originally refers to a medieval trumpet known for its sharp and piercing sound. When used metaphorically, it signifies an unmistakably compelling call. In a biblical context, a clarion call is a summons from God or one of His prophets urging people to respond, repent, or take specific actions.

Here are a few biblical examples of clarion calls:

Isaiah 58:1: "Cry aloud, do not hold back; lift up your voice like a trumpet; declare to my people their transgression, to the house of Jacob their sins."

Clarion Call: Isaiah is commanded to loudly and clearly call out the people's sins, urging them to recognize their wrongdoings and repent.

Joel 2:1: "Blow the trumpet in Zion; sound the alarm on my holy hill. Let all who live in the land tremble, for the day of the Lord is coming. It is close at hand."

Clarion Call: Joel is instructed to sound an alarm to warn the people of the imminent and significant event—the coming of the day of the Lord. This is a call to preparedness and repentance.

Revelation 3:20: "Here I am! I stand at the door and knock. If anyone hears my voice and opens the door, I will come in and eat with that person, and they with me."

Clarion Call: This verse is a personal invitation from Jesus to individuals, inviting them to open their hearts and lives to Him—a compelling call to relationship and communion with Christ.

Ezekiel 33:7: "Son of man, I have made you a watchman for the people of Israel; so hear the word I speak and give them warning from me."

Clarion Call: God appoints Ezekiel as a watchman whose duty is to listen to God's words and warn the people. This call is a call of vigilance and responsibility.

Matthew 28:19-20: "Therefore go and make disciples of all nations, baptizing them in the name of the Father and of the Son and of the Holy Spirit, and teaching them to obey everything I have commanded you. And surely I am with you always, to the very end of the age."

Clarion Call: Known as the Great Commission, this is Jesus' call to His disciples to evangelize the world, teaching and baptizing in His name. It's a clear and urgent mission given to all believers.

In each example, the clarion call is undeniable in its urgency and clarity. It demands a response from those who hear it. The call serves as a powerful reminder of the responsibilities and actions expected by God.

OUR PRESENT-DAY CLARION CALL

Today, we face our own clarion call—a call to avoid the spiritual consequences of neglecting our responsibilities.

Imagine going to the mailbox and taking out a large envelope, a summons from God—a divine lawsuit.

For years, in workshops and teachings, we have quoted to audiences of youth leaders, parents, teachers, and pastors, "My people are destroyed for lack of knowledge," but perhaps what we haven't considered is that our ignorance, or worse, our rejection of knowledge, is destroying the next generation.

Hosea 4:6 begins with, "My people are destroyed for lack of knowledge…" This verse is often interpreted to mean that a knowledge deficit leads to destruction.

That interpretation seems to make sense, right?

Let's read Hosea 4:6 together:

> My people are destroyed for lack of knowledge: because thou hast rejected knowledge, I will also reject thee, that thou shalt be no priest to me: seeing thou hast forgotten the law of thy God, I will also forget thy children.

Upon closer examination, we see that it is not merely a lack of knowledge but a rejection of it that leads to devastating consequences. When knowledge is rejected, understanding is clouded, and discernment is lost.

Hosea 4 speaks directly to us as leaders, warning that the spiritual state of one generation can be traced back to the actions or inactions of the previous generation. This understanding is a sobering reminder of the impact of truth suppression. When leaders fail to fulfill their responsibilities, the next generation suffers.

THE LAWSUIT FROM GOD

What do we do when Yahweh brings charges against us?

Hosea 4:1-4 reads:

> Hear the word of the LORD, you Israelites, because the LORD has a charge to bring against you who live in the land: "There is no faithfulness, no love, no acknowledgment of God in the land. There is only cursing, lying and murder, stealing and adultery; they break all bounds, and bloodshed follows bloodshed. That is why your land is in mourning, and everyone is wasting away. Even the wild animals, the birds of the sky, and the fish of the sea are disappearing. Don't point your finger at someone else and try to pass the blame! My complaint, you priests, is with you.

We encourage rereading this scripture while holding a handheld mirror.

After reading this scripture and looking myself in the mirror, I want to sit under a tree and repent.

The passage goes on to describe the dire consequences of rejecting God's truth: "There is no faithfulness, no love, no acknowledgment of God in the land. There is only cursing, lying, and murder, stealing and adultery; they break all bounds, and bloodshed follows bloodshed."

This indictment is chilling, especially when we reflect on our own culture today. We see the evidence all around us—

Clarion Call

corruption, violence, and moral decay. Profane language has become the norm, even within Christian communities. Cursing and cussing are corrupt communication, but it is often posted and celebrated by youth. And for the record, S***, A**, F***, and W*** T** F*** are profane, corrupt communication. Yes, we have to name it because many Christians are defending the right to use similar words on stage at church and as a regular part of a Christian lifestyle—which is another form of rejecting the truth.

People who know us might think, "You guys are hard on yourself; you do a lot in the community to help the next generation."

Our response is: Have you turned on the news and scrolled social media lately?

My wife and I have reached a milestone: we're now at an age where the students we teach could easily be our children. During a class we facilitated with about 40 college students, this realization hit home.

An 18-year-old student approached us with a request to host a teenage Bible study, and we found ourselves engaged in a back-and-forth conversation, initially assuming that our students were surely not teenagers and questioning why she would want a teen-branded bible study on a college campus.

Then we realized we'd been overlooking the passage of time, almost ignoring our birthdays. The age gap between our college students and us has widened to the point where it's tangible, where the thought of them being our children isn't far-fetched anymore. We could have a kid in college. WOW!

We have even more of a responsibility to help train a

child in the way he or she should go so that when he or she is old, he or she will not depart from it.

For the last twenty years, we have felt like we are raising kids (who are not our own) through the programs, workshops, and classes we've been teaching. We feel very much a part of the village and responsible for the outcome of what we see.

As leaders, our rejection of truth has led to a society where theft, divorce, gun violence, teen pregnancy, bullying, abortion, school shootings, teen violence, mass shootings, cyberbullying, and murder are at record highs.

The statistics are alarming: globally, about 464,000 people die from homicide each year, and youth homicide rates in some regions are skyrocketing (United Nations Office on Drugs and Crime. *Global Study on Homicide 2019*. United Nations, 2019, https://www.unodc.org/documents/data-and-analysis/gsh/Booklet1.pdf).

RESPONSIBILITY FOR THE NEXT GENERATION

As leaders, parents, and educators, we have around 18 years to ensure that the next generation does not suffer due to our neglect. Hosea 4:6 warns us that the consequences of our failure to impart knowledge and faith are severe. If we fail to pass on our spiritual legacy, the next generation may become disconnected from God, inheriting the consequences of our inaction.

Consider a relay race: if the first runner fumbles the baton, the entire team suffers, regardless of how well the others run. Similarly, if we neglect to pass on our faith, the next generation inherits the consequences, potentially leading to their disconnection from God.

Or imagine setting out on a road trip without checking the fuel gauge. If one person forgets to fill the gas tank, everyone ends up stranded, facing the consequences of that oversight. In the same way, our failure to nurture and educate our youth spiritually can leave them unprepared and vulnerable.

It is our responsibility to ensure that we equip the next generation with the knowledge and faith they need to stay connected to God. We must not allow our neglect to be the reason they suffer. As darkness looms over many young people we encounter, we must remember that darkness is healed with light. We are called to share the light, embrace the light, and be the light.

NO YOUTH, NO CHURCH SOULUTIONS

4
CONSTRUCTION

In recent years, many of us have observed (with growing concern) that numerous churches struggle to lay the necessary groundwork for a thriving youth ministry. This shortcoming often makes young people feel disconnected and unengaged, precisely when they need guidance and support most. The importance of a solid foundation cannot be overstated, whether building a house or nurturing the spiritual growth of our youth. This chapter addresses these critical issues and offers a blueprint for change.

We wholeheartedly know that many churches face challenges. To be protected and effective, a youth ministry must have clear direction, cohesive values, structured organization, strong leadership, and engaging programs. Without those things, a youth ministry can be vulnerable and ineffective.

However, we are not without hope. By carefully examining the essential elements of our youth ministry, we can create an environment where young members feel valued, understood, and inspired. We can lay the groundwork for a ministry that not only endures but flourishes, becoming a cornerstone of support and guidance.

Imagine a youth ministry with a clear vision and mission that resonates with every member, a set of core values that guide every decision, a well-organized structure that ensures smooth operation, strong leadership that mentors and inspires, and dynamic programs that engage and uplift. This is not just a dream but a tangible reality within our reach.

As we construct a robust youth ministry foundation, let us carry a spirit of hope and determination. Together, we can build something significant—an enduring ministry that profoundly impacts the lives of our young people and stands the test of time.

PARENTS

Let's be clear: if you don't have parents, you don't have a youth ministry.

Everyone talks about "these parents." Parents aren't doing this; parents aren't doing that. The complaints are endless. But, for many churches. The pandemic revealed the strength or lack thereof with parents.

What do we mean?

Many churches have allowed parents to drop their kids off at youth groups, V.B.S. (Vacation Bible School), children's churches, or other youth functions without prioritizing building a relationship beyond "That's Jason's mom, I think."

This is our seven-step plan to ensure parents show up, show out, and be an asset to your ministry. The clue to the secret lies within the acronym P.A.R.E.N.T.

P: Plan

Think of parents as jugglers, constantly balancing work, home, and their children's activities. Imagine Sarah, a mother of three, navigating between soccer practice, piano lessons, and school events. Now, add church activities to her already packed schedule. Creating a well-thought-out plan that accommodates their busy lives will make it easier for parents like Sarah to participate. Offer flexible scheduling, clear communication, and advanced notice of events. This level of planning shows we understand their challenges and respect their time, and makes your church activities a feasible part of their routine.

A: Address Their Needs and Objections

Parents can sometimes be seen as "Debbie Downers," expressing concerns or objections. However, it's essential to see these moments as opportunities. Take, for instance, John, who always seems to have a complaint about youth group activities. Instead of dismissing him, invite him to share his thoughts. By listening to their concerns and seeing things from their perspective, we demonstrate empathy and a genuine willingness to understand and address their issues. This level of intentionality helps resolve concerns, builds trust, and opens lines of communication.

R: Respect

Respect goes beyond mere politeness; it's about genuine engagement. Imagine hosting a monthly "Parent's Forum," where parents can voice their thoughts and actively participate in decision-making. Respect their opinions, even if they differ from yours, and show appreciation for their contributions. When parents feel respected, they are more likely to reciprocate with support and involvement.

E: Engage Them

Because we don't want to underutilize your amazing parents. Instead, we're dreaming big with a Parent Expo and Roundtable, which is kind of like a super cool booster club for your ministry.

Parents are very busy, so they need a transparent system to plug into. We've got to plan and prepare ahead of time because, let's be honest, if we don't, they might eat us alive! But don't worry about that—we'll have everything in order and ready to roll.

Picture this: parents with extraordinary talents, brilliant ideas, and fantastic connections all come together to help you. They'll be brainstorming, fundraising, and figuring out exactly what you need to make your youth ministry the absolute best. It's like having a team of champions cheering you on and helping you reach new heights. Let's get your parents pumped up and show them how their involvement can turn your dreams into reality!

N: No to Negativity

Negativity can be contagious, especially in close-knit communities. Picture a youth ministry meeting where a frustrated parent's complaints bring down the entire group's morale. To counter this, focus on maintaining a positive environment. Celebrate small wins, recognize contributions, and provide support for parents. These actions create a culture where positivity thrives, and will make your church a welcoming and uplifting place for everyone.

T: Teamwork Makes the Dream Work

Building a sense of teamwork is crucial. Consider organizing events that require collaboration between parents and church leaders, such as family retreats or community service projects. When parents like Darryl and Jossalyn see themselves as part of a team working towards a common goal, it fosters a sense of belonging and cooperation. Encourage open dialogue and shared responsibilities, emphasizing that the success of the church community depends on everyone's participation.

SURVEY PARENTS

Understanding the types of parents in your congregation is essential. Conduct surveys to gather insights into their preferences, challenges, and suggestions. Are they new parents like Crystal and Micky looking for support and guidance? Or are they seasoned parents like Michael and Latoya, who can offer valuable experience and mentorship? Tailor your approach based on these insights to effectively meet their specific needs.

PUTTING IT ALL TOGETHER

Following this P.A.R.E.N.T. Plan will create an environment where parents feel valued, respected, and integral to the church community. They'll be more likely to show up, actively participate, and become assets to your ministry. Remember, the key is to see parents as partners on this journey, working together to create a thriving and supportive church environment for everyone.

Implementing the P.A.R.E.N.T. Plan fosters a robust and engaged community of parents who feel valued. This foundation is crucial as we align our efforts with our church's vision and mission.

Parents are not just participants; they are crucial to realizing our goals. We create a unified front by addressing their needs and integrating their contributions. This unity propels us forward, allowing us to fulfill our mission more effectively.

Let's begin crafting a vibrant vision and mission to excite and energize our parent volunteers. Our commitment to planning, respect, positivity, and teamwork isn't just about attraction; it reflects the core values driving our church's purpose.

Together, we'll explore creating a compelling vision and mission that resonates with parents and inspires unity. Let's make our vision and mission something parents can rally behind, and fuel their passion and dedication.

Proverbs 29:18-19, states, "Where there is no vision, the people perish: but he that keepeth the law, happy is he."

What if things change because you choose to see it change? In a previous chapter, we highlighted that God will exceed our thoughts or imagination (Ephesians 3:20).

We know your church wants to change the narrative of your ministry. We see it in your eyes (pun intended). We see that you want to go from mediocre to good, and from good to great. We know you are looking at what other ministries are doing down the street and getting discouraged when you start to compare.

Consider not getting caught up in the hype of another church, what they are doing, and what you are not doing. Yes, be inspired by other ministries, but we should refrain from competing for the next generation for bragging rights. The real battle is against an agenda to contaminate the next generation through media, music, and mania. Know what God has called you to do in the kingdom. Every church has its own "oil."

The Blue Church is anointed to do what they do, and the Green Church is anointed to do what they do.

Have you considered there's a reason you are in the community you are in?

Just like every person has a working genius, every church has a genius—meaning a set of gifts that supports what God would have you do in your city concerning the next generation.

We love what Myles Munroe says about vision and purpose. He states, "Vision and purpose tell you what to do and what not to do."

When we know our lane, we know which lanes to stay out of. We all are in the business of spreading the Gospel and making disciples, but how we contribute to that in our local assembly will vary. Every church doesn't have a gym; some ministries are in rural areas, while others are in the city. It is essential to craft a mission and vision statement that will keep you grounded as you navigate with your "ingredients."

MISSION AND VISION

Mission

A mission statement explains why an organization exists and how it will serve its stakeholders. In our case, it will describe how we will serve our children, youth, and teenagers—our students. It is the starting point for your strategy, goals, and objectives. The mission should be no more than one or two sentences and should clearly explain what your youth ministry does and who you're doing it for.

Below is the No Youth No Church mission statement:

No Youth No Church Mission Statement: We help churches quickly discover their unique ability to become the top youth ministry in their city.

To have an effective mission statement, spend some time thinking about:

1. **Why?** Why is what we're doing necessary?

2. **What?** What problem or pain point are we solving? What do we do? What is the benefit?

3. **How?** How are we different? Who are we reaching? The statement should be clear, simple, and specific.

Let's review the No Youth No Church mission. It's a single sentence.

1. *Who are we helping?* Churches.

2. *What service are we providing?* Discovery.

3. *Why?* To help churches become the top youth ministry—reaching more youth. It's a single 17-word sentence.

This next tip is often overlooked but critically important: the youth ministry mission should be aligned with the church mission and shared throughout your church. Most churches have a mission statement. The youth ministry mission statement should sound like a derivative of the church mission statement. If your church is equipping the community, your youth ministry should be equipping the youth of the community in some form. The youth ministry should echo the church.

Construction

Now that you have your mission statement, you can create:

1. Measurable goals and objectives
2. Youth ministry strategy
3. A plan to get help and funding

   Note: A solid mission statement explains your purpose, and people are more inclined to support a cause that resonates with them and that they understand.

Vision

The vision is what we want to become. It is a declaration of our aspirations. What has God told us or shown us we will be?

Our vision is also the bridge between mission and strategy. More on strategy later. For now, every youth ministry should create a strategic plan annually and reviewed at least quarterly. The vision statement is our guardrail. If a proposal does not match the vision, we should not do it. Our vision statement provides the big picture of where we want to go, and the strategy details how we will get there.

The vision statement inspires, unites people around a common goal, and clarifies strategic decisions. Every decision should be apparent in light of the vision.

Vision statements are typically shorter than mission statements, but not always. They should be memorable, feasible, and aspirational. Vision statements should stretch us, making us a little nervous and excited at the same time. They should also be invigorating and represent our best, indicative of all we want to become if there were no hindrances.

Questions to answer to help you get there:

1. What problem do we need to solve?
2. What is our dream end state?
3. Who do we want to serve?

Vision statements should be unique, ambitious, expressive, and brief.

Check out the No Youth No Church vision statement.

Vision Statement: To become the premier platform for churches in the Black community struggling to keep youth engaged.

Again, a simple 16-word single sentence that attempts to leave no question as to why we're here. It's aspirational. We're not there yet, but it's where we will be. We want to be synonymous with solutions for youth engagement in the church, particularly the Black church. We want leaders to think of us when they need help and creative insight to build their youth ministry and to attract and retain youth in their churches.

Another common example:

Apple's Vision: To make the best products on earth and to leave the world better than we found it.

Apple's Mission: To bring the best user experience to customers through innovative hardware, software, and services.

Has Apple lived up to its vision and mission?

We'd submit that whether you're Team iPhone or Team

Construction

Android, smartphone technology would not be where it is today without Apple's innovation in the late 1990s and early 2000s.

Take some time to answer the questions in this chapter and hone in on who you want to become, what you want to accomplish, who you want to help, and who you are called to serve.

What is the Lord impressing upon your heart?

How will your community, your country, and the world be different because you lived?

NO YOUTH, NO CHURCH SOULUTIONS

5
CALCULATED

Ready to learn a French phrase? The is *mise en place*. No, I'm not speaking in an unknown tongue—chefs and cooks already know this phrase. *Mise en place* is a French culinary term that means "everything in its place."

The term refers to the practice of setting up all the necessary ingredients, tools, and equipment before actually starting to prepare a meal. This method helps chefs streamline the cooking process, save time, increase efficiency, and reduce the risk of mistakes or accidents in the kitchen. By having everything organized ahead of time and within reach, the cook can focus on the task at hand and ensure that each recipe step is executed correctly.

Mise en place is an essential part of any professional kitchen and a valuable practice for home cooks like me who want to improve their skills—I can be the worst when it comes to prep!

However, I want to use this concept as an analogy. Consider for a moment that restaurants represent youth ministries, chefs are the youth leaders, and *mise en place* is what every youth ministry should have as part of its culture and daily practices.

In my opinion, the lack of *mise en place* hurts our youth ministries nationwide. *Mise en place's* presence—or absence— will be evident in any youth department. Every action in youth ministry requires *mise en place*.

Encourage your team to start incorporating this term into your discussions. Yes, even consider learning the word like a song and singing it around the office or in team meetings. Leaders can illustrate the benefits of *mise en place* by emphasizing the importance of being well-prepared and avoiding last-minute stress. After all, youth teams that spend little time planning are quickly exposed, as youth can tell when something is thrown together.

BEGIN WITH THE END IN MIND

Stephen Covey wisely advises, "Begin with the end in mind."

This principle is not just a strategy for business or personal goals; it's a timeless truth that can shape every aspect of our lives. It's a call to envision the outcome before we start, to see the destination before we take the first step. This mindset echoes the wisdom of Proverbs 24:27: "Prepare your work outside; get everything ready for yourself in the field, and after that, build your house."

Envision planning a youth event or a Sunday school lesson. Like an engineer meticulously plans every detail before breaking ground on a new project, we must thoughtfully prepare our hearts and materials before diving in. This approach ensures that when we gather for a team meeting, children's church, or even a revival, we are not just reacting to the moment but are guided by a clear vision of what we hope to achieve.

An "engineer mentality" means anticipating challenges, gathering the right resources, and building a solid foundation. It's about being calculated and intentional, understanding that the success of our choir rehearsal or worship night isn't just about the time spent together but the preparation that went into it. When we organize a V.B.S., we don't aim to fill the schedule but to create lasting memories and impart deep spiritual truths.

Preparation in the field represents doing the groundwork. It's about getting everything ready, setting up for success, and ensuring all the tools, people, and plans are in place. This level of preparation is the fruit of being calculated. It's the assurance that when the children arrive, the songs are sung, and the prayers are lifted; everything flows seamlessly because the groundwork has been laid.

So, let's embrace this wisdom. Whether we're organizing a team meeting, leading a revival, or teaching a Sunday school class, let's prepare our work outside. Let's prepare everything in the field and then build our house with confidence and clarity. Preparing will ensure our efforts bear fruit, grounded in thoughtful preparation and a clear vision for the future.

When a team displays frustration and events are more stressful than enjoyable, it often indicates poor planning or no planning. These types of environments are avoidable.

Example Checklist for a Calculated Youth Ministry Team

The following checklist can serve as inspiration. However, please create a thorough checklist in your youth ministry manual or handbook.

1. **Define Clear Objectives:**

    - **Children's Church:** What spiritual lessons or values do you want to impart each week?

    - **Youth Conferences:** What key takeaways or skills do you want the youth to acquire?

    - **Weekly Youth Ministry Events:** What is the specific goal of each event (e.g., community building, spiritual growth, fun and engagement)?

2. **Plan the Logistics:**

    - **Venue:** Ensure the space is appropriate for the activity and number of participants.

    - **Schedule:** Create a detailed agenda with times for each event segment.

    - **Materials:** List all needed materials (e.g., Bibles, crafts, games, audio-visual equipment).

3. **Prepare the Team:**

    - **Roles and Responsibilities:** Assign specific tasks to each team member.

    - **Training:** Provide necessary training or briefings to ensure everyone is equipped to fulfill their roles.

    - **Communication:** Establish clear lines of communication before, during, and after the event.

4. **Anticipate Challenges:**

    - **Contingency Plans:** Prepare backup plans for potential issues (e.g., bad weather, technical difficulties). See more on this later in the chapter.

- **Safety Measures:** Ensure all safety protocols are in place and communicated to the team.
- **First Aid:** Have a first aid kit and a plan for emergencies.

5. **Create Engaging Content:**

    - **Lesson Plans:** Develop engaging and age-appropriate lesson plans that align with your objectives.
    - **Activities:** Plan interactive activities that reinforce the lessons and encourage participation.
    - **Worship and Music:** Choose songs and activities that resonate with the youth and enhance the experience.

6. **Promote the Event:**

    - **Marketing:** Use social media, church announcements, email lists, flyers, and personal invitations to spread the word.
    - **Registration:** Set up a straightforward and easy registration process for participants.
    - **Reminders:** Send reminders leading up to the event to ensure good attendance. Use text messaging platforms for quicker engagement.

7. **Engage with Parents and Guardians:**

    - **Communication:** Keep parents informed about the event's purpose, schedule, and requirements.
    - **Involvement:** Encourage parental involvement

where appropriate, such as volunteering or attending sessions.

8. **Evaluate and Reflect:**

    - **Feedback:** Gather feedback from participants, parents, and team members to understand what worked and what didn't. We will go deeper here in a minute.

    - **Review:** Hold a debriefing session with the team to discuss the event's successes and areas for improvement.

    - **Documentation:** Keep records of the plan and what actually happened for future reference.

9. **Follow-Up:**

    - **Thank You Notes:** Send thank-you messages to volunteers, speakers, and participants.

    - **Next Steps:** Provide resources or suggestions for participants to continue their spiritual growth.

    - **Planning for the Future:** Use the feedback and evaluations to start planning the next event with the end in mind.

COMMON PRINCIPLES FOR ALL EVENTS:

- **Clear Objectives:** Always start with a clear understanding of what you want to achieve.

- **Detailed Planning:** Comprehensive logistics and agenda planning are crucial.

- **Team Preparation:** Ensure every team member

knows their role and is adequately prepared.

- **Engaging Content:** The core content should always be engaging, relevant, and spiritually enriching.
- **Effective Communication:** From promotion to post-event follow-up, clear and consistent communication is critical.
- **Safety and Contingency Planning:** Always prioritize safety and have backup plans ready.
- **Evaluation and Reflection:** Continuously seek feedback and strive for improvement.
- **Parent and Guardian Involvement:** Keep them informed and engaged in the process.

By following this checklist, you can cultivate a calculated approach that ensures each event is meaningful, well-organized, and impactful. This preparation reflects the wisdom of beginning with the end in mind, setting the stage for success and growth in your youth ministry.

CONTINGENCY PLANS

"Without counsel plans fail, but with many advisers they succeed" (Proverbs 15:22).

Let's talk about one of the most underrated exercises in church. If we overlook it for the adults, it's likely non-existent in youth ministry: contingency planning! Brainstorming what could go wrong, calculating the probability of the incident occurring, assessing the impact, and pre-identifying the mitigations we will employ to address said incidents are not the most fascinating exercises for most. In fact, most would rather watch paint dry. Yet, this can be the least desirable aspect of event planning and arguably the most important, especially when we're planning events for youth and children.

Enter the FMEA. If you haven't had much exposure to the engineering or manufacturing worlds, you've likely never heard of this term. An FMEA, or Failure Mode and Effects Analysis, is typically used in industrial applications to mitigate potential failures in processes, products, and systems. Completing a robust FMEA could be the difference between life and death. Hopefully, that's an exaggeration for a youth ministry event, but having one could prove indispensable when faced with the unexpected.

By definition, we've already considered the solution. An FMEA gives us an advantage in ensuring the safety, security, and, ultimately, the success of your event.

So, how does it work?

The first step is identifying the challenges or what could go wrong—these are the failure modes. In this part of the exercise, everyone has permission to be a "Debbie Downer." We want and need to identify as many potential failure modes as possible. We want to hear the bad news from every angle.

What happens if it rains?

What will we do if a child gets sick, or God forbid a child goes missing?

How will we handle a power outage or if the sound guy doesn't show up?

What is the impact of volunteers or teachers not showing

up, and does that increase the likelihood of safety issues?

What if we arrive at the church and it's locked, and the person who's supposed to open the church is running late for youth choir rehearsal?

You get the idea, but most of these are real examples. We need to put everything on the table and live in a worst-case-scenario world, but only temporarily. Thankfully.

Then, assess the impact if something does go wrong.

We may end up with a list of 20 things, but there will likely be themes. For example, the mitigation for a child becoming sick or spraining an ankle may be similar. However, a child breaking a leg may call for a different response.

Take the time to consolidate the list to avoid the exercise becoming overwhelming and creating a list that is so long that no one reviews it. Also, keep in mind that the effect of safety concerns is wildly different from logistics.

Now comes the fun part. We get to assign a score to the items we just identified.

Once we have identified what could go wrong, it's time to rank these items based on severity (or how bad a problem is), likelihood of occurrence (how often the problem will happen), and ease of detection (can we see and perhaps even prevent the problem from even occurring) These are the "S," "O," and "D" columns of the FMEA, respectively.

Once we have scored our items, we can identify our priorities, recognize gaps, and address significant weaknesses.

Proverbs 22:3 states, "A prudent person foresees danger and takes precautions. The simpleton goes blindly on and suffers the consequences."

This tool supports our ability to practice prudence. It is game-changing and a must-have for every youth ministry.

Don't worry; we've included an example of an FMEA so you can create a template for your events.

Be creative—this is your opportunity to think through your "what if" scenarios and determine the appropriate responses. Mitigations may differ by organization. For instance, if the person responsible for opening the church is notorious for being late, do we anticipate that and assign the task to more than one person or relieve him of those duties altogether? That person may be better suited elsewhere, where timeliness is less critical. The FMEA gives you a quantitative tool to make those decisions.

As you plan, we implore you to consider a more severe example: if you are taking your youth on a field trip, please prepare for worst-case scenarios and plan accordingly. Some things are true accidents and are unavoidable, but at a minimum, the youth pastor and their delegate should know emergency contact information, allergies, health information, and medications. Remember, the youth are entrusted to your care, so you must be prepared.

I know this is a serious topic, but ensuring our precious children's safety is necessary.

Remember, the FMEA is not a one-and-done tool. Once the event (or whatever we're using these strategies for) ends, we must assess how it went.

Did we follow the plan?

Did something unexpected happen?

Or was it flawless because we anticipated what could go wrong and solved the problem before it occurred?

That's next level! The FMEA is a game-changer that helps you continuously improve and get incrementally better. Remember, this is not a sprint; it's a marathon.

END OF CHAPTER ACTION:
STEPS FOR AN EFFECTIVE FMEA SESSION

The Failure Modes and Effects Analysis (FMEA) can be conducted in person or via Zoom (although in-person meetings are preferred).

The core team typically consists of three to five members, though more can be included if necessary. The key is to ensure the team members are subject matter experts and decision-makers. You will need both a facilitator and a note taker. Err on the side of fewer participants, as too many can lead to inaction and inefficiencies, and this task is too important to result in a stalemate.

Diverse points of view are also essential. You don't want everyone to be from the youth choir; make sure you have representation from other ministries that may not be directly involved in youth ministry but will show support. Ministries such as the culinary/kitchen ministry, the greeters (ushers), or the parking lot ministry are good places to start.

Step 1: Gather the Crew

Ensure that key team members can attend. Everyone's voice must be heard. If you plan to work the event as a leader, you should be at this session.

Step 2: Identify the Risks

Identify what could go wrong. Nothing is off the table. Here, you have permission to be negative and think about worst-case scenarios. Remember, it's for a good cause—our preparation!

Step 3: Assess the Impact

Now that we've listed all the risks, take some time to assess how severe they are in comparison to each other. Our list will likely range from "not bad" to "catastrophic." However, the facilitator should ensure that everyone must participate in this exercise. Score the impact on a scale of 1, 3, or 5 (1 = low, 3 = moderate, 5 = high).

Step 4: Rate the Likelihood

Evaluate each risk and make a judgment call on how likely it is to occur. Is this a rare, "struck by lightning" type event, or is it something more familiar that could realistically happen? Score the likelihood on the same scale: 1 = low, 3 = moderate, 5 = high.

Step 5: Calculate Risk Priority

Multiply the impact score by the likelihood score for each risk the team identified. This information will give us the priority score. With this, we can quantitatively prioritize which risks to tackle first. Only some things require the same amount of time and focus. The team will have identified where we need to focus your attention first.

Step 6: Plan, Prepare, Prevent

This step is a twist on the traditional "Plan, Prepare, Perform." Now that we have a list of things that can go wrong, think through prevention. For example, consider how to handle a person with temporal issues, as mentioned earlier.

Step 7: Do a Retro

We'll delve into retrospectives a little later, but for now, understand the importance of a post-event analysis. How often do you spend time after an event or service to discuss what went well and what didn't?

This action is often called a post-mortem in project management, but since our events are about life, we'll call it a retrospective. In other words, we're looking back for ways to continuously improve.

Simple Modified Example

RISK	IMPACT (1, 3, 5)	LIKELIHOOD (1, 3, 5)	Priority (Impact / Likelihood)	ACTION PLAN
What if it rains during our outdoor event?	5	5	25	Develop a rain plan - date, location, time, speaker, food, notifications, etc.
What if a child breaks his/her leg?	5	*	*	*Systems and processes are key. Do you have onsite, on-call medical personnel? How will the parents be notified? Do you have emergency contact information on every child? Think through and document all emergency procedures. Ensure you have waivers and indemnification in place as well. Please seek the advice of professional medical and legal services.
What if Brother John is late again?	5	5	25	Proposal: Reassign Brother John to another task and have two people with keys to open the church.

Table 1. Risk, Impact, Likelihood
*Likelihood depends—is the event a worship night or are you bungee jumping at a youth event?

THE RETROSPECTIVE

Ret·ro·spec·tive - looking back on or dealing with past events or situations.

In a business context, especially in software development, it's a team meeting where the objective is to review and analyze an event, project, or process with the expectation of making it better the next time.

Few tools are as effective as a "retro" when assessing a past event or project and making recommendations for the future. If you want to learn from the past and avoid repeating mistakes, then a retro is a tool you should add to your toolkit.

HOW DOES IT WORK?

First, set the framework. Let's pretend you just completed your first youth conference. Inform your team that you will be meeting to discuss the conference and that they should come prepared to discuss what went well, what could have been done differently, and how the second annual youth conference can be improved.

Preferably, conduct this exercise in person. A room with a whiteboard works best, but a white wall or a sticky flip chart will suffice. Use Post-It Notes in at least four different colors. Designate a color for each section outlined below. For example, "What did you Learn" - yellow Post-It Note, "What did you Lack" - green Post-It Note, "What did you Love" - pink Post-It Note, and "What do you want to Leave" - blue Post-It Note. Give everyone a Post-It Note of each color.

This is a modified version of a common framework

called the 4L's, originally developed by Mary Gorman and Ellen Gottesdiener, adapted for our context. Use these questions to evaluate our pretend youth conference:

What did you Learn?

- What were our strengths as a team?
- What were our weaknesses as a team?
- Did any processes or systems create problems for you during the youth conference? If so, what and how?
- What did you learn that will make the next youth conference better or easier?

What did you Lack?

- What resources do you wish you had (or had more of)? How would they have made a difference?
- What does success look like for the conference?

What did you Love?

- Did anything go better than you expected? If so, what?
- What tools, techniques, and/or resources helped you during the youth conference?
- What was our superpower during the youth conference?
- What can we be proud of as a team?

Calculated

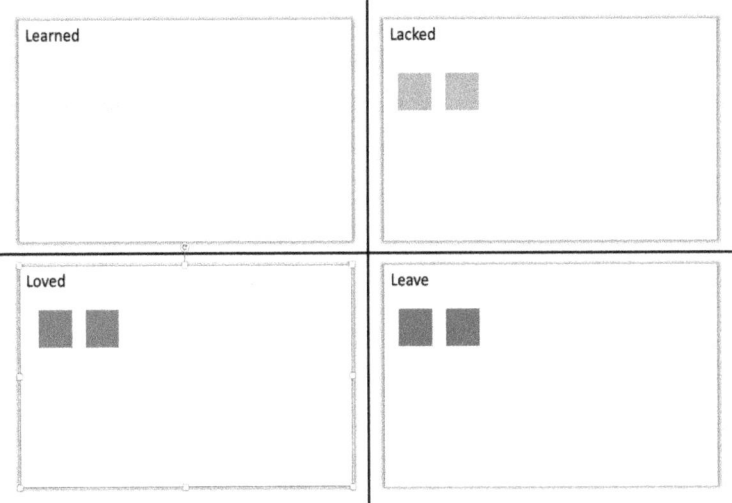

Table 2. Learned, Lacked, Loved, Leave

What do you want to <u>Leave</u>?

- Did anything happen during the youth conference that caught you off guard?

- What do you definitely NOT want to see at the next youth conference?

- How can we improve the overall process(es) that we used?

- What's still unresolved about our process(es) or an issue?

- If you could go back and change one thing about the youth conference, what would it be?

Before starting the session, ensure you have created a safe environment. Every team member should be encouraged to participate. Comments are fair game as long as they are respectful, not derogatory or incendiary.

Of course, pointing fingers and playing the blame game is counterproductive. This session should be candid and transparent, and the team should be empowered to share even unpopular opinions.

Assign a facilitator to moderate and ensure the discussion doesn't get stuck on a single topic, as there will be a lot to cover. One way to avoid going down a rabbit hole is to create a "parking lot"—a list of discussion points requiring deeper review than the time in the session allotted. Items on this list may also require a smaller, more focused group or even research or data collection for the conversation to be fruitful.

Don't be afraid to table a discussion, but assign an owner, set a follow-up date, and schedule the follow-up. Ensure everyone is aligned with the expected outcomes.

As you proceed, start with each section and allow everyone to write their answers to the questions. We've provided several sample questions, but feel free to create your own to supplement them. Give the team ample time to think through the questions for each section and post their sticky notes on the whiteboard or wall.

Once each section is complete, discuss it. Here are a couple of keys to success:

1. **Egos and Pride Are Not Welcome:** This exercise intends to improve us all. It can be somewhat therapeutic, so be prepared for real conversations.

2. **Create an Action Plan:** The worst thing a team can do is have a great discussion, reach a consensus on what needs to change, and have a clear vision on how to elevate the ministry—and then do nothing. Don't be that youth

ministry! You have the tools to be effective, responsive, and make a real difference in your community. Be accountable to God, each other, the senior pastor, and your students. They are worth it.

NO YOUTH, NO CHURCH SOULUTIONS

6
CAPTAIN

VISIONARY LEADERSHIP IN YOUTH MINISTRY

Effective strategy in youth ministry hinges on visionary leadership. In a world where countless influences compete for the attention of our youth, strong leadership is not just desirable; it's essential.

As John Maxwell's Law of the Lid suggests, the potential of our youth ministry can only rise as high as its leadership. This type of leadership isn't confined to the youth pastor; it extends to the entire church's pastoral team.

Visionary leadership is about steering the ministry in a direction that empowers the next generation to thrive. Reflect on who's at the helm of your youth ministry—their vision and passion are the catalysts that will propel our mission forward.

THE ESSENTIAL ROLE OF THE FRUIT OF THE SPIRIT

In the fast-paced environment of youth ministry, a leader who embodies the Fruit of the Spirit is invaluable.

The Apostle Paul, in his letter to the Galatians, outlines these virtues: love, joy, peace, patience, kindness, goodness, faithfulness, gentleness, and self-control (Galatians 5:22-23). These are not abstract qualities. They are practical tools that every effective youth ministry leader must wield to navigate the unique challenges of guiding volunteers, engaging with energetic youth, and collaborating with church leadership.

Youth ministry is dynamic, with challenges as varied as they are demanding. Leaders often balance the enthusiasm of lively youth, the dedication of busy volunteers, and differing perspectives among church leadership. In this context, the Fruit of the Spirit becomes a vital toolkit, enabling leaders to create a cohesive, supportive, and spiritually enriching environment.

Love: The Foundation of Ministry

Love is the cornerstone of effective leadership. It compels leaders to see beyond immediate frustrations and focus on each individual's intrinsic value and potential. When a volunteer is late, or a child is disruptive, a leader grounded in love responds with understanding and grace, creating an atmosphere where everyone feels valued and respected.

Joy: Cultivating a Positive Atmosphere

Joy in leadership goes beyond a cheerful demeanor; it creates an environment where positivity and enthusiasm are contagious. This joy can uplift the team, making the ministry a place of refuge and excitement, even amidst the chaos of planning and execution.

Peace: Navigating Conflicts with Grace

Peace is crucial when conflicts arise, whether among team

members or with church leadership. A leader who embodies peace can navigate disagreements calmly and composedly, seeking resolutions that promote harmony and understanding.

Patience: Enduring Through Challenges

Patience is one of the most tested virtues in youth ministry. Leaders must remain patient with volunteers juggling numerous commitments, youth testing boundaries, and church leaders with different priorities. This patience ensures steady progress, even when it feels slow.

Kindness and Goodness: Building Trust and Integrity

Kindness and goodness build a foundation of trust and integrity. Leaders who consistently act with these virtues earn the respect and loyalty of their team, fostering a culture of mutual support and ethical conduct.

Faithfulness: Demonstrating Commitment

Faithfulness is reflected in a leader's unwavering commitment to their calling and those they serve. This steadfast dedication inspires confidence and motivates others to invest fully in the ministry's mission.

Gentleness: Leading with Compassion

Gentleness involves approaching situations and individuals with compassion and understanding. A gentle approach can de-escalate tensions and encourage open, honest communication.

Self-Control: Maintaining Balance

Self-control is essential for maintaining balance in the face of stress and temptation. A leader who practices self-control can set appropriate boundaries, manage their time effectively, and model a balanced life for their team and the youth.

A STORY OF TESTING AND TRIUMPH

Consider Shirley, a youth ministry leader who faced significant challenges during a critical church event. The annual youth retreat was fast approaching, and tensions were high. Volunteers were stretched thin, and the youth were more rambunctious than usual because they were excited about the upcoming trip. To complicate matters, the church deacon, typically supportive, expressed strong reservations about the retreat's expenses.

One evening, a heated argument erupted between two essential volunteers over the retreat's logistics. As voices escalated, Shirley felt her patience wearing thin. She took a deep breath, drawing on her inner reservoir of peace and self-control. Instead of reacting impulsively, she approached the volunteers with gentleness, acknowledged their concerns, and guided the conversation toward a constructive solution. Her kindness and understanding defused the tension, leading to a compromise that satisfied everyone involved.

Later, Shirley met with the deacon, listening respectfully to his concerns. Responding with love and faithfulness to the ministry's vision, her joy in the mission and steadfast commitment eventually won him over, and he agreed to support the retreat.

Through these challenges, Shirley's embodiment of the Fruit of the Spirit resolved immediate conflicts and strengthened the team's unity and trust. Her leadership turned a potentially disastrous situation into a testament to the transformative power of spiritual virtues in action.

BALANCING LEADERSHIP IN YOUTH MINISTRY

THE ROLE OF THE YOUTH LEADER

My wife and I have had the privilege of conducting youth workshops across our region, and through these experiences, we've come to appreciate the vital role of the youth leader deeply. Much like the captain of a ship, the youth leader steers the course, ensuring the ministry reaches its destination safely and successfully.

However, one significant challenge we've noticed repeatedly is youth leaders' tendency to assume or take on too many roles, especially in smaller churches. While multitasking is often done out of necessity, it can harm the ministry and its participants.

THE CHALLENGE OF BEING OVERWHELMED

In many smaller churches, resources are limited, and staff are often stretched thin. It's common to see a single individual wearing multiple hats—youth leader, worship coordinator, Sunday school teacher, and even church treasurer. While this dedication speaks volumes about their commitment, it also highlights a critical issue: the risk of becoming too busy to lead effectively.

THE DANGER OF HAVING TOO MANY IRONS IN THE FIRE

When a youth leader is spread too thin, they struggle to devote the necessary time and energy to each role. This lack of focus can lead to several issues:

1. **Burnout**: Juggling too many responsibilities can quickly lead to physical, emotional, and spiritual exhaustion. A burnt-out leader cannot effectively inspire or guide their team and the youth.

2. **Ineffective Leadership**: Constant multitasking may result in missing important details, failing to plan adequately, or neglecting essential aspects of the ministry. Multitasking can lead to poorly organized events, miscommunication, and a general sense of disarray.

3. **Neglect of Relationships**: Building meaningful relationships with the youth and volunteers is crucial for a thriving ministry. However, an overwhelmed leader may need help to invest in these relationships, leading to a lack of trust and connection within the team.

4. **Sabotaging the Ministry**: Ultimately, a leader who is too busy to lead effectively can inadvertently undermine or sabotage the ministry they are passionate about, which can affect the youth and the morale and cohesion of the volunteer team.

We've met youth leaders who are incredibly passionate but visibly exhausted, struggling to keep up with their commitments. We've listened to volunteers express their frustrations over unclear direction and lack of support. We've even witnessed youth feeling disconnected because their leader is constantly preoccupied with other tasks.

Imagine a youth leader named Marcel who was responsible for organizing church events, managing the Sunday school curriculum, and overseeing the church's social media. Marcel was dedicated and capable but found himself overwhelmed by his multiple roles. He was constantly putting out fires instead of proactively leading his team, causing his volunteers to feel unsupported and the youth group to start dwindling.

What if Marcel realized the importance of focusing his energy on his primary role as a youth leader?

What if he delegated some of his other responsibilities and prioritized building relationships within his team and with the youth?

Over time, a remarkable transformation would occur. Marcel's renewed energy and attention would rejuvenate the youth group, and his team would feel more empowered and engaged.

THE IMPORTANCE OF FOCUSED AND EFFECTIVE LEADERSHIP

Our experiences have taught us that the health of a youth ministry depends significantly on the leader's ability to balance the vision, their health, and delegation.

VISION AND INTEGRITY

Strong leaders are defined not only by their roles but by their commitment to a clear vision. As leaders in youth ministry, we must articulate this vision clearly and consistently.

Just as a ship needs a steady hand, our ministry thrives when every member, from volunteers to youth participants, understands and works towards a shared purpose.

PERSONAL HEALTH AND BALANCE

We've also learned that leadership effectiveness is closely tied to personal health. It's not just about eating an apple or making sure our water intake is appropriate, especially during events; it's about maintaining a sustainable lifestyle. Planning with regular exercise, proper nutrition, and sufficient rest allows us to consistently bring our best selves to youth activities. This approach enhances our physical well-being and strengthens our mental, emotional, and spiritual resilience.

DELEGATION AND TRUST

One of the pitfalls we've observed in many youth ministries is the temptation for leaders to become "solo leaders" or "Red Bull leaders."

These individuals often feel they must do everything themselves, fearing that delegation equates to losing control. However, effective leadership is about trusting and empowering others.

Delegating tasks to capable team members lightens our load and fosters a sense of ownership and commitment among volunteers. Building trust through training and clear communication ensures our team members feel valued and capable, ultimately strengthening the ministry.

Consider the Biblical account of Jethro's advice to Moses. In Exodus 18, Jethro, Moses' father-in-law, observed Moses becoming overwhelmed by his numerous responsibilities in leading the Israelites. Jethro advised Moses to delegate some of his duties to capable leaders, allowing him to focus on the most important tasks. This wisdom lightened

Captain

Moses' load and improved the overall leadership structure.

Now, think back to the story of Marcel, the youth leader overwhelmed by his multiple roles. Just like Moses, Marcel found himself constantly putting out fires rather than proactively leading his team. His volunteers felt unsupported, and the youth group started to dwindle.

If we find ourselves in a similar situation as Marcel, we can take Jethro's advice to heart. Focus your energy on your primary responsibilities and delegate other tasks to capable team members. Prioritize building relationships within your team and with those you lead. Doing so can lighten our load and create a more empowered and engaged team, just as Marcel did. This approach can lead to remarkable transformations, renewed energy, and a more vibrant community

Reflecting on Jethro's timeless advice and Marcel's experience, it's clear that focused and effective leadership involves understanding your strengths and knowing when to delegate.

Therefore, it's paramount that youth leaders recognize their limits and prioritize their primary role. By doing so, they can lead with clarity, purpose, and inspiration, building a vibrant and dynamic ministry.

Over the years, we've gained insights from others and expanded on our learning. Some of the most profound learning we acquired speaks to effective leadership. Max DePree stated, "The first responsibility of a leader is to define reality. The last is to say thank you. In between, the leader is a servant."

DePree's words highlight the critical role of leaders in being realistic about their capabilities and the needs of their ministry. They also underscore the importance of servant leadership. Similarly, Tony Blair said, "The art of leadership is saying no, not yes. It is very easy to say yes."

Blair's insight is particularly relevant for youth leaders in smaller churches, where the pressure to take on multiple roles can be intense. Learning to say no and focusing on one's primary responsibilities is necessary for effective leadership. Finally, Jeroen De Flander shared, "You cannot be everything to everyone. If you decide to go north, you cannot go south at the same time."

Flander's quote expresses the importance of focused leadership. Trying to fulfill too many roles simultaneously can dilute our effectiveness.

As my wife and I reflect on our journey and the countless workshops we've conducted, one message stands clear: a youth leader must be the captain of their ship, navigating with focus and intent.

While the temptation to take on multiple roles is strong, especially in smaller churches, it's critical to remember that being too busy to lead can sabotage the very ministry we're trying to build.

By embodying the Fruit of the Spirit and focusing on their primary calling, youth leaders can steer their ministry toward success, creating a lasting impact on the lives of the youth they serve.

Activity: Use the framework below to identify the type of leader you are and the type of team you have. Gather the team and ask them to:

- List your top 3 strengths.

Captain

- List your top 3 weaknesses.
- List things that frustrate you.
- Identify and describe your personality type.
- Rate your patience 1-10 (10 being the highest).
- Rate your creativity 1-10 (10 being the highest).

7
CREW

Finding and recruiting the right team members takes time and energy, but having a fully engaged and high-functioning team is crucial for the health and success of your youth department. Once you've got the right people in place, it's vital to determine how to use them and best align their skills and interests.

A team in sync needs a solid plan to execute effectively. As it says, "Write the vision, make it plain, so everyone can read it and run with it" (Habakkuk 2:2). This ensures everyone is on the same page, ready to work together seamlessly toward the ministry's goals.

When your team is cohesive and well-aligned, the youth ministry can hit its stride. When everyone knows their role and understands how their unique skills fit into the bigger picture, they're more motivated and efficient. This kind of teamwork fosters innovation, boosts problem-solving, and leads to a more dynamic and impactful ministry. Investing in your team's development and ensuring a clear vision unites them is essential for keeping your youth ministry thriving.

Lastly, it's important to recognize your team's capacity

and plan honestly and realistically. This grounded approach is critical to successfully transforming your vision into reality.

C.A.P.A.C.I.T.Y.

It's common for youth ministry teams to aspire to hold multiple events—sometimes as many as 17 or more in a year. Some of these events are larger in scale than others. We've noticed that many of the events are tied to holidays within the quarter. For example, Americans have dozens of holidays.

There's Black History Month, Martin Luther King Jr., Valentine's Day, and Presidents' Day in the first quarter of the year. In the second quarter, we have Easter Sunday, Juneteenth, Cinco de Mayo, Earth Day, Mother's Day, and Memorial Day. The third quarter has Independence Day (4th of July) and Labor Day. In the last quarter, churches often host events around Columbus Day, Fall Festivals, Veterans Day, Thanksgiving Day, Christmas Day, and New Year's Eve.

If a ministry schedules events for every holiday, that's over 17 events in 12 months. When you add a desire to do an annual youth conference, youth revival, graduation celebration, block party, VBS and other outings, there is a potential for events that should take tons of planning every week.

What's my point?

When a ministry attempts to tackle 17 or more events in a year, it often leads to burnout and diminished quality. The illusion of constant activity can blind a ministry into believing that busyness equates to effectiveness, even if the events are not executed with excellence.

Crew

I often encounter ministries, especially those in a relaunch or revamp phase, that try to preserve events that yield little to no results. This may stem from a desire not to offend the creator of an event or to maintain tradition. However, assessing which events provide a meaningful return on investment (ROI) is essential. Some traditional events may need to be reignited or reimagined, but a judgment call must be made on what stays and what goes. Consider juxtaposing your youth event against the Capacity Mnemonic as you make that decision. I like to call it the "CAPACITY Check."

C—Can we do it, and should we do it?

1 Corinthians 10:23 says, "I have the right to do anything," you say—but not everything is beneficial. "I have the right to do anything"—but not everything is constructive. Whether you should do something and can do something should be scrutinized and placed under a microscope.

My dad always says, "Count up the cost."

We encourage youth ministries to carefully evaluate whether they should undertake an event by counting the costs. Count up the cost of volunteers, supplies, time, food, marketing, admin work, post work, and time for fasting and praying for the event.

A—Are we at least two deep in manpower or staffing for each area?

Leviticus 26:8 states, "Five of you will chase a hundred, and a hundred of you will chase ten thousand, and your enemies will fall by the sword before you."

C.S. Lewis said, "Two heads are better than one, not because either is infallible, but because they are unlikely to go wrong in the same direction."

Most Broadway plays have a backup person (an understudy), so that if anything goes wrong, the show can go on.

We know that flat tires, sickness, emergencies, accidents, and even death happen at the worst times. While having two people in every area is ideal, if you don't have at least one backup, you fail in the A of the capacity checklist. It's better to solve problems with two heads—mistakes are easily caught when two people are on the job.

P-Proper people placement

How is our delegation quality?

In the words of Dr. Sam Chand, "Proper people placement prevents problems."

Similarly, Jim Collins emphasizes the importance of getting the right people on the bus.

As leaders, we can quickly assess whether the right or wrong people are on the team. This understanding doesn't mean the person is bad or wrong; it just means they aren't the right fit for this job.

Traditionally, we've politically kept people in positions they weren't qualified. Pastor Travis Greene of Forward City said it best at a No Youth, No Church retreat: "The thing worse than no help is the wrong help."

I'm sure I'm not the only one who's been frustrated with individuals who dropped the ball in areas I trusted them with.

Delegating tasks to someone who doesn't have the capability is a recipe for disaster. Not making the right choice will lead to mistakes, missteps, mismanagement, and a bad reputation.

A—Answers for objections and the vision

People who provide critical feedback aren't bad. We all know the church member, team member, or leader who brings a dose of *"We can't do that, what about this, do we have enough money?"* and so on.

Sometimes, these people aren't seen in a good light; they're viewed as negative, pessimistic, and focused on the downside of any situation.

On the contrary, that level of thinking is a blessing in disguise. Worst-case scenario thinking is good for risk management. My wife says, "Debbie Downers just need permission to be one."

I suggest taking notes when people offer critical feedback—they'll highlight problems before they grow into big ones and help with influencing change.

C—Contingency Planning

A Failure Modes and Effects Analysis (FMEA), discussed in a previous chapter, is a systematic method used to evaluate and mitigate potential risks in a process, product, or system. This structured approach helps organizations proactively address issues before they escalate.

By implementing a thorough FMEA and a robust contingency plan, you can turn these "Debbie Downer" moments into invaluable opportunities for growth and preparedness. Those who often voice concerns, like the proverbial Debbie Downer, are not to be dismissed but embraced. Their foresight and attention to detail can elevate minor problems before they escalate, leading to meaningful improvements.

I—Identify individuals to serve in every area.

In any youth ministry, having individuals serve in every area is crucial for effective management. Ensuring all important roles are filled allows for smooth operation and success in various events, rehearsals, and meetings. Each activity, regardless of its nature, demands the involvement of dedicated people who are clear on their responsibilities. This clarity comes from well-structured plans, courtesy calls, clear communication of vision, and consistent follow-ups. These elements ensure that each individual knows their role and performs it effectively.

Dr. Asa Don Brown stated, "Communication is the lifeblood of any organization. Without it, the structure falters, the purpose blurs, and the goal fades into the background."

Proper communication is essential in every aspect, from planning to execution, and it ensures everyone is on the same page.

The entire structure can collapse if every role in the youth department is not filled. Events may become disorganized, important details overlooked, and the overall experience for the youth can and often does suffer. This can lead to a decline in participation and enthusiasm, ultimately hindering the ministry's mission.

Furthermore, team members need adequate training and preparation time for their assignments. Proper training equips them with the necessary skills and knowledge, while thorough preparation ensures they are ready to handle their tasks confidently. When team members are well-prepared, they contribute more effectively, leading to a more successful and impactful youth ministry.

T—Time management

Time management is critical for any team, especially in a youth ministry where team members often juggle multiple responsibilities. In small churches, this challenge is even more pronounced due to the limited number of volunteers and staff. Each person may be involved in several aspects of the church's operation, from leading worship and teaching Sunday school to organizing events and providing pastoral care.

William Penn once said, "Time is what we want most, but what we use worst."

Waiting until the last minute to put things together can have severe effects on the team and the youth ministry as a whole. Last-minute planning leads to stress, mistakes, and a lack of professionalism, which can diminish the quality of events and activities. This disorganization not only affects the team's morale but also impacts the youth, who may feel the effects of a poorly executed program. It can result in lower attendance, disengagement, and a loss of trust in the ministry's ability to provide meaningful and enriching experiences.

To avoid these pitfalls, here are some quick suggestions for effective time management:

1. **Prioritize Tasks:** Identify the most important tasks and tackle them first. Use the Eisenhower Matrix to categorize tasks by urgency and importance.

2. **Create a Schedule:** Develop a detailed schedule that outlines all tasks and deadlines. Use tools like Google Calendar or Microsoft Outlook to keep track of commitments.

3. **Use Time Management Tools:**

    - **Asana or Trello:** This system is for project management and task tracking
    - **To-do List:** This method is used to create and manage items that need to be completed.
    - **Slack:** This platform can be used for team communication and collaboration.

4. **Delegate Responsibilities**: Distribute tasks among team members according to their strengths and availability. Ensure everyone knows their role and deadline.

5. **Set Reminders:** Use digital reminders and alarms to keep track of deadlines and important milestones.

6. **Regular Check-ins:** Hold brief, regular meetings to review progress, address any issues, and adjust plans as needed.

7. **Avoid Procrastination**: Encourage team members to start on tasks early and break larger projects into smaller, manageable steps.

Here's a simple checklist to help manage time effectively:

1. **Define the Objective:** Clearly outline what needs to be accomplished.
2. **List Tasks:** Break down the objective into specific tasks.
3. **Assign Deadlines:** Set realistic deadlines for each task.
4. **Allocate Resources:** Identify what resources are needed and who will be responsible.
5. **Monitor Progress:** Regularly check on the status of tasks and adjust as necessary.

6. Review and Reflect: After the event or project, review what worked well and what could be improved upon the next time.

Y—Yielded to God

In ministry, you're going to need more than skill and time management. You need God! Some of the greatest mistakes I've seen in my years of working with youth ministries across the country come from leadership that forgets this is God's business, not theirs.

We're caretakers and stewards of God's work. Matthew 16:18 says, "Upon this rock, I will build my church, and the gates of hell shall not prevail against it."

But 1 Peter 5:8 reminds us that the enemy prowls around like a roaring lion, seeking whom he may devour. Youth ministry is no exception to this. Youth pastors need to be on alert and recognize the spiritual warfare at play.

A strong connection with God ensures that leaders are guided by divine wisdom and strength rather than relying solely on human abilities.

Yielding to God in ministry is a continual process of surrendering personal ambitions and agendas to align with God's will. It involves seeking His guidance through prayer, worship, and the study of scripture, trusting that He will provide the direction and resources needed to fulfill the ministry's mission.

"Unless the Lord builds the house, they labor in vain who build it" (Psalm 127:1). This passage emphasizes the importance of relying on God's strength and wisdom in all ministry endeavors.

Yielding to God means trusting Him fully, including trusting the unique gifts and contributions He has bestowed upon each team member. God has intricately knitted your team together, with each person playing a vital role. Being comfortable in our skin and confident in the abilities God has given us is crucial for the success of the youth ministry.

Embrace your strengths and trust that God has placed you in this ministry for a purpose.

The Bible provides numerous examples of how seeking God can lead to extraordinary outcomes. When King Jehoshaphat faced a vast army, he sought God's guidance and led his people in prayer. As a result, God delivered them from their enemies (2 Chronicles 20). Similarly, when the early church prayed together, they received the Holy Spirit's power, which enabled them to spread the gospel with boldness and effectiveness (Acts 4:31).

Let these examples encourage you. Your youth ministry can thrive by seeking God's guidance, trusting in His plan, and relying on prayer. Remember, God has a purpose for us; together, we can achieve great things for His kingdom.

Stay rooted in His Word, seek His face continually, and trust that He will lead you in the right direction.

Joshua 23:10 reads, "One can chase a thousand," so imagine how many five people can put to flight. In other words, we can accomplish a lot when we have the right help.

As a leader or team member, what type of people are on your team? Do you know your team? Do you know their birthdays, anniversaries, living conditions, and how many kids they have? Thessalonians 5:12 encourages us to "know those who labor among [us]."

Truly knowing an individual is an intimate and detailed process. However, knowing these details will pay off.

BUILDING A TIGHTER TEAM
EMBRACING THE WISDOM OF 1 THESSALOIANS 5:12

In 1 Thessalonians 5:12, the Apostle Paul writes, "And we ask you, brethren, to know those laboring among you, and leading you in the Lord, and admonishing you."

This scripture calls us to a deeper understanding and appreciation of those who work alongside us in ministry. It urges us to move beyond superficial interactions and truly get to know our team members. Building unity and intimacy that strengthens our collective efforts.

The word "know" in 1 Thessalonians 5:12 is translated from a Greek word that means to remember and appreciate. This highlights the importance of recognizing and valuing the contributions of all team members. Appreciating and remembering these contributions fosters a culture of mutual respect and understanding. It ensures that every team member feels valued and heard, which is essential for a cohesive and effective team. Acknowledging and appreciating the critical insights from all voices strengthens the team's ability to navigate challenges and achieve success.

To build a tighter, more cohesive team, we must embrace several practices that allow us to live out the wisdom of this verse. These activities help us learn about each other, perceive and understand our unique strengths and weaknesses, and create a supportive and intimate community.

Praying Together: Praying together is a powerful way to connect spiritually. It allows us to share our burdens, hopes, and gratitude, creating a bond that transcends everyday interactions. When we pray together, we become more aware of each other's struggles and victories, leading to a deeper understanding and empathy. This practice strengthens our relationship with God and fortifies our connections with one another.

Eating Together: Sharing meals is one of the simplest yet most effective ways to build fellowship. When we break bread together, we engage in meaningful conversations and learn about each other's lives beyond the scope of ministry. These moments of fellowship help us understand the personalities and stories that shape our teammates, making us more aware of who they are and what they bring to the table.

Fellowshipping through Recreational Activities: Engaging in recreational activities allows us to see our teammates in different contexts, highlighting various aspects of their personalities and talents. Whether it's a game night, a hike, or a casual outing, these activities help us perceive and appreciate our team's diverse skills and qualities. They also provide opportunities for relaxation and fun, which are essential for maintaining a healthy and balanced ministry life.

Worshiping Together: Worshiping together unites us in a common purpose and reinforces our shared faith. As we sing, pray, and reflect on God's word as a team, we extend grace where needed and are encouraged by each other's journey.

Sharing Personality Tests: Personality tests can be an insightful tool for understanding each other's strengths, weaknesses, and working styles. By sharing and discussing the results, we learn how each person operates and perceives the world. This awareness helps us to communicate more effectively, assign tasks that align with individual strengths, and support each other in areas of weakness. Understanding these dynamics creates a sense of appreciation and respect, enhancing our teamwork.

By incorporating these practices, we fulfill the call of 1 Thessalonians 5:12 to "know those laboring among you." We move beyond surface-level interactions to truly understand, perceive and appreciate each other. This awareness allows us to behold the unique contributions of each team member and pay attention to their needs and strengths. As a result, our team becomes more intimate, unified, and effective in our shared mission.

In essence, these activities help us build a ministry team that is not only functional but also deeply connected. By praying, eating, fellowshipping, worshiping, and understanding each other's personalities, we create a supportive and cohesive environment where everyone feels valued and understood. This leads to a tighter, more resilient team capable of achieving great things together.

Finding and recruiting the right team members takes time and energy. However, having a highly functioning team with invested members matters immensely to the health and success of your organization or ministry.

Once the right members are in place, understand how to leverage and align their skills and interests.

In like manner, a team, on one accord, needs a strong plan in place in order to execute effectively. As a second reminder, "write the vision, make it plain," so they can read and run it (Habakkuk 2:2).

NO YOUTH, NO CHURCH SOULUTIONS

Think about a youth ministry team where each member not only understands their strengths and weaknesses but also appreciates those of their colleagues. Just like the 16 personality test helps individuals understand their unique traits, Patrick Lencioni's Working Genius framework takes it a step further for teams.

In this ministry, Sarah thrives in Wonder, constantly dreaming up innovative ways to engage youth with creativity and passion. She generates innovative ideas for events and programs that resonate deeply with the community. Meanwhile, David excels in Tenacity, meticulously organizing schedules and ensuring every event runs smoothly. His attention to detail and structured approach ensures the team is prepared, on schedul, and in budget.

Understanding these natural inclinations frees team members to operate in areas that give them the most fulfillment. When roles align with these inherent talents, individuals find their work deeply satisfying, making their contributions more impactful.

Conversely, the framework explains why some team members might feel frustrated with specific tasks. For instance, Emma, who prefers Enablement, feels fulfilled when mentoring and supporting youth volunteers. However, she finds herself frustrated when tasked with detailed logistical planning, which aligns more with David's Tenacity genius.

Recognizing and respecting each team member's Working Genius helps build roles and responsibilities that play to their strengths. It ensures that tasks are delegated in a way that maximizes efficiency and minimizes frustration.

It's important to note that while the Working Genius

framework offers valuable insights into team dynamics and roles, it's essential to approach any organizational model with a discerning eye. While Patrick Lencioni's expertise is respected in the business world, it's always wise to consider how these principles align with your team's values and beliefs, particularly in settings like youth ministry.

By harnessing the power of the *Working Genius* alongside a deep understanding of individual strengths and weaknesses, youth ministry teams can create a culture of collaboration, fulfillment, and impactful service to their community.

THE SMALL TEAM DILEMMA

It seems like every time we talk about successful church ministries, we hear about the importance of having a well-rounded team. Experts rave about the benefits of a group that knows its strengths and weaknesses, understands its dynamics, and operates like a well-oiled machine. But what happens when the reality of our situation doesn't match this ideal?

For many of us, our ministry teams are small—too small to dive into the complexities of team dynamics and working genius. We struggle with limited manpower and resources, finding it nearly impossible to get into the nuts and bolts that make a team click. We read about large churches with their dedicated youth events, elaborate setups, and extensive support systems, and it feels like a distant dream.

How can we even begin to organize youth events when our team is stretched so thin?

We find ourselves in a frustrating loop. We want to do more, but our limited capacity holds us back. Expectations feel heavy, and the burden of trying to do everything with so few hands often leave us feeling defeated. How can we make an impact when we can barely manage the basics?

ENTER COLLEGE STUDENTS: THE UNTAPPED RESOURCE

Amid these struggles, there is a silver lining—college students. Often overlooked, these young adults are not just potential attendees but can be invaluable contributors to our ministry. College students bring energy, fresh perspectives, and a willingness to serve that can reinvigorate even the smallest teams. By involving them in our ministries, we can tap into a powerful resource that can help us overcome the limitations of our small teams.

College students can provide the extra hands needed to plan and execute youth events, bring new ideas to the table, and help create a vibrant, dynamic environment that attracts more young people. They are at a stage where they are eager to make a difference and can often dedicate time and energy that older team members might struggle to find.

We can transform our small, struggling teams into effective, thriving ministries by embracing this untapped resource. College students can help bridge the gap between our current capabilities and ministry goals, providing the support and enthusiasm needed to make our visions a reality. Involving them is not just a stopgap solution; it's a strategic move that can lead to long-term growth and success.

So, instead of lamenting our small numbers, let's consider the potential waiting to be unlocked in our local colleges and universities. By investing in college students, we can build a stronger, more capable ministry team that can tackle the challenges we face and create meaningful, impactful youth events. Let's focus on this incredible resource and watch as our ministries flourish and grow beyond what we ever thought possible.

VALUING CASH, COMMUNITY, CAUSE, AND CARE FOR COLLEGE STUDENTS

College students highly value four key elements: cash, community, cause, and care. Each plays a critical role in their lives, especially when balanced with their educational and personal development.

Cash: Financial stability is essential for college students, many of whom juggle part-time jobs and academic responsibilities. Earning $15 an hour can significantly ease their financial burdens, covering basic expenses like tuition, books, and living costs. This wage provides a sense of security, enabling students to focus more on their studies and personal growth rather than financial stress. Moreover, churches hiring college students for special projects can benefit from fresh, creative ideas, especially in social media management, graphic design, event planning, and content creation. For example, a marketing major can help design promotional materials, while a communications major can enhance the church's online presence through strategic social media campaigns.

Community: Being part of a supportive community helps students feel connected and engaged. Whether through clubs, organizations, or church groups, a strong community provides emotional support and a sense of belonging. Notably, a survey conducted by the American College Health Association in 2020 found that 63% of college students felt very lonely at some point within the past year. Partnerships between colleges and organizations like the Fellowship of Christian Athletes (FCA) can build connections, and enrich students' college experiences.

Cause: Many college students are driven by a desire to make a difference. They value being part of causes that align with their beliefs and passions. Engaging in meaningful activities through organizations like FCA allows students to contribute to something larger than themselves.

Additionally, many college students need community service hours for their academic programs, and churches can benefit from this need by involving students in various service projects. This mutual benefit helps churches get help with their initiatives while providing students with the required hours.

Care: Emotional and spiritual care is vital for students' well-being. Access to resources and support systems, including mentorship and counseling, helps students navigate the challenges of college life. Churches and organizations partnering to provide this care can significantly impact students' health and success. Additionally, when churches demonstrate genuine care for college students, they cultivate loyalty and commitment. A college student who feels valued and supported by their church community is more likely to prioritize attending services and participating in church activities. This loyalty creates a strong bond between the student and the church, leading to long-term engagement and service.

In summary, investing in college students is a win=win for both the youth ministry and the students. By hiring college students for projects related to their fields of study, churches support students financially and gain innovative contributions that enhance their ministry. Additionally, by offering community service opportunities, churches can help students fulfill their academic requirements while advancing their own missions.

Building a thriving youth ministry hinges greatly on the strength of the team involved. As Ronald Reagan once wisely remarked, "The greatest leader is not necessarily the one who does the greatest things. He is the one that gets the people to do the greatest things."

A cohesive and committed team can achieve remarkable feats in nurturing young minds and hearts.

Patience is key when assembling your dream team. As Nelson Mandela famously said, "It always seems impossible until it's done."

Take the time to select team members who share the vision and are dedicated to the mission. Each step forward, no matter how small, contributes to the larger goal of transforming lives through faith and community.

In the words of Mother Teresa, "I can do things you cannot, you can do things I cannot; together we can do great things." Collaboration and unity within the team are essential. Consider every recommendation with thoughtful prayer and assessment, implementing changes in manageable, bite-sized pieces. This approach ensures that each initiative is rooted in purpose and aligns with your ministry's overarching goals.

Remember, as Martin Luther King Jr. once said, "Faith is taking the first step even when you don't see the whole staircase." Trust in the process of building your team and advancing your ministry. With dedication, patience, and faith, your youth ministry can impact the lives of young people and the community at large.

8
CREATIVITY

As leaders, it's common to use innovation and creativity to reach the lost. However, this can be a sensitive topic. Our position is encapsulated in a phrase we coined years ago: "Trends that don't bend."

This statement means we embrace new approaches, but they must always align with our core biblical values and faith.

The Bible reminds us in Romans 12:2, "Do not conform to the pattern of this world, but be transformed by the renewing of your mind."

This verse emphasizes the importance of staying true to our spiritual convictions while engaging with the world. We understand that God would never want us to promote evil to promote good. Philippians 4:8 encourages us to focus on what is true, noble, right, pure, lovely, and admirable. These are the standards we uphold in our mission and ministry.

Our goal is to innovate without compromising our faith, ensuring that our actions and messages reflect God's love and truth in all we do. Creativity is a game-changer in youth ministry, and here's why it matters: teaching style, communication, promoting events, collaboration with youth, harnessing creativity, and impact.

Teaching Style: Being creative in how we teach can make a significant difference. When we use interactive activities, multimedia, and hands-on experiences, lessons become more engaging and memorable. It's all about capturing their interest and helping them connect with the material.

Communication: How we communicate with young people is key. Creative approaches like social media, videos, or relatable stories can make our messages hit home. It's about meeting them where they are and speaking their language while conveying that God has a language, too.

Promoting Events: Creativity can make a significant impact when it comes to getting the word out about events. Unique themes, eye-catching promotions, and engaging content can excite and motivate youth. We live in an era where it's easier than ever to create or outsource quality promotional content at little to no cost.

Collaboration with Youth: Creativity is subjective, and everyone sees it differently, which is a good thing. By collaborating with young people on creative projects, we enrich our ministry and give them a chance to shine and feel included. Embracing diverse creative ideas requires openness and a willingness to explore new perspectives. Encourage youth to bring their unique talents and ideas, whether in music, art, drama, or other forms of expression.

Harnessing Creativity: As we work with youth, it's essential to harness their creativity while remembering our guiding principle of "Trends That Don't Bend."

Therefore, we celebrate their innovative ideas while

Creativity

ensuring they align with our core values. We must be patient and understanding, recognizing that young people may sometimes express themselves in unconventional or even offensive ways. Rather than being quick to reprimand, we should seize these moments as teaching opportunities. We can guide them in understanding how to present their creativity through a kingdom lens, transforming raw ideas into powerful expressions of faith.

Impact: When we recognize creativity as subjective, we create an environment where young people feel valued and empowered. This collaboration builds a sense of belonging and encourages them to contribute their gifts to the community. By allowing youth to express themselves creatively, we enhance our ministry and inspire them to take ownership of their faith journey. Be prepared for serendipitous results— this approach often leads to unique and inspiring outcomes that enrich our ministry and build up the next generation.

Creativity isn't just a nice thing to have— it is essential for making teaching, communication, and event promotion effective and exciting.

OBJECTIONS

Not everyone is on board with investing in innovation and new ways of thinking. To prepare you for those *sometimes* uncomfortable conversations, let's review a few of the objections and consider possible responses.

Objection 1: "Creativity takes too much time and resources."

Response: It's true that creativity can require extra effort, but the payoff is worth it! Investing time and resources into creative approaches often leads to more engaged and excited youth. Plus, you don't have to go big every time—small creative tweaks can make a significant difference and might even inspire others to get involved.

Objection 2: "Not everyone will appreciate or understand creative methods."

Response: Creativity is subjective, and that's okay! While not everyone may connect with every creative idea, the goal is to reach as many people as possible in ways that resonate with them. By trying different approaches, you'll find what works best and can continuously adapt to meet diverse needs.

Objection 3: "It's hard to balance creativity with the core message."

Response: Creativity and the core message can go hand in hand! The key is to ensure that creative methods enhance, rather than overshadow, the core message. When thoughtfully integrated, creativity can make the message more compelling and memorable, helping to reinforce what's most important.

Objection 4: "My team isn't very creative."

Response: Creativity isn't necessarily something you're born with; it can be developed and nurtured. Encourage your team to explore new ideas and experiment with different approaches. Sometimes, it takes a little inspiration and support to unlock their creative potential. And remember, even small steps can lead to big changes!

Objection 5: "We don't have a budget for creative projects."

Response: Creativity doesn't have to be expensive! Plenty of low-cost or even free resources are available, like online

Creativity

tools and community collaborations. Sometimes, the most impactful creative ideas come from thinking outside the box with what you already have. Plus, creativity often leads to innovative solutions that don't break the bank.

EMBRACING TECHNOLOGY

Embracing creativity may come with challenges, but with the right mindset and encouragement, it can lead to incredible results and a more vibrant, engaging ministry. Later in this chapter, we'll provide examples of "low-hanging fruit" to guide your creativity. In today's world, with the internet and AI, creativity just got simpler.

Embracing technology and AI isn't just a trend; it's essential for staying relevant and impactful in youth ministry. The digital world is here to stay, and integrating these tools can unlock endless creative possibilities—from interactive apps and virtual reality to AI-driven content. By streamlining routine tasks and communications, technology allows us to focus on meaningful engagement with the youth, working smarter rather than harder. It also expands our reach beyond geographical limits through social media, podcasts, and videos, connecting us with young people wherever they are.

Embracing tech and AI builds a culture of innovation, pushing us to think outside the box and stay dynamic. Plus, it shows that we understand the digital landscape young people navigate daily, making our messages more relatable and impactful. In essence, diving into the tech and AI world transforms how we engage, innovate, and connect with the youth, offering an opportunity to enhance our impact and inspire the next generation.

As we continue our mission to ignite and equip the next generation, we focus on practical strategies that can be implemented today. Let's explore some "low-hanging fruit" that can transform your ministry and enrich the lives of young people.

A CALL TO INNOVATE

EMPOWERING THE NEXT GENERATION WITH "TRENDS THAT DON'T BEND"

In a world filled with noise and endless demands, we recognize the challenge and necessity of reaching the next generation with the truth of the Gospel. As leaders, we have the privilege and responsibility to innovate and create without losing sight of our core values. Our guiding principle, "Trends That Don't Bend," encourages us to champion new methods while remaining steadfast in our faith. We stand firm in our belief that God calls us to influence the world without conforming to it.

PEDAGOGY: TEACHING WITH PURPOSE AND PASSION

Our approach to teaching is grounded in the timeless wisdom of Scripture. Romans 12:2 urges us to "be transformed by the renewing of your mind," reminding us that true transformation comes from aligning our thoughts with God's truth. We aim to create learning experiences that resonate with young hearts and minds, cultivating a deep understanding of faith that equips them to face the world with confidence and conviction.

Creativity

1. **Biblical Wisdom & Modern Relevance:** We use the framework of "Wings and Wisdom," combining engaging discussions with biblical teaching to make learning both relevant and impactful.

2. **Interactive Learning:** Our style is interactive and dynamic, drawing from our "Emoji Praise and Worship Game" to encourage participation and joy in discovering God's Word.

3. **Empowerment Through Knowledge:** We believe in empowering youth by providing them with tools for critical thinking and spiritual growth. Our "Youth 52" curriculum is designed to inspire a lifelong journey of faith.

EVENTS: CREATING EXPERIENCES THAT TRANSFORM

Our events are crafted to provide more than just entertainment; they are opportunities for transformation and growth. We invite you to explore the potential of our "low-hanging fruit" events, designed to engage and inspire the youth:

1. **Bible and Basketball:** This event blends the excitement of sports with the depth of Bible study, promoting fellowship and spiritual growth on the court.

2. **The Scoop:** An ice cream social that creates a welcoming environment for open dialogue and teaching, making faith accessible and enjoyable.

3. **Praise, Preaching, and Prizes:** A lively event featuring music, dynamic preaching, and fun giveaways, all aimed at drawing young people closer to God.

4. Gospel Grill: An outdoor gathering centered around good food and Gospel music, encouraging community and celebrating our faith.

INCORPORATING OUR STYLE INTO YOUR CULTURE

We invite you to make this approach a part of your culture. Let it shape how you engage with the youth, creating an environment that reflects the vibrancy and depth of your faith. To see our teaching style in action, visit our social media platforms, especially YouTube, where you can witness these innovative strategies firsthand.

Let's embrace the call to lead with courage and creativity, equipping the next generation to stand firm in their faith and shine as lights in the world.

READY TO GO DEEPER?

Next, we'll walk through the details of five "low-hanging fruit" events that you can implement in your youth ministry immediately. These ideas are designed to be straightforward and cost-effective, allowing you to focus on building relationships and sharing the Gospel. Feel free to remix these ideas or let them spark creativity in your team.

Bible and Basketball:

Description: Combine the excitement of a casual basketball game with the inspiration of a Bible study. This event requires minimal setup—a basketball court and a few volunteers to lead the study. Start with a short Bible lesson or discussion, then head to the court for some fun and fellowship. The relaxed environment encourages youth to open up and discuss faith while enjoying a favorite pastime. Make sure to have a follow-up plan to connect with the students afterward, such as inviting them to a weekly youth group or a follow-up game night.

Why It's Easy: It requires minimal setup—just a Bible, a basketball, and a court. It combines physical activity with spiritual growth, making it engaging for participants.

Impact: It balances faith and fun, encouraging spiritual discussion and physical activity. It's a great way to build relationships and keep everyone active and connected. Don't have a basketball court? Make it a Tandem Youth Ministy (TYM) event. More on TYM later.

Wings and Wisdom

Description: Host an event where attendees enjoy wings while discussing a topic related to wisdom or personal growth.

Why It's Easy: This event is simple to organize—you just need a venue, wings, and a discussion topic. It encourages casual conversation and learning, creating a welcoming atmosphere where youth can explore biblical teachings on wisdom in a way that relates to their lives. Quality matters, so consider inviting a guest speaker or using multimedia to enhance the discussion. To keep the momentum going, offer a series, create a custom devotional, or use a hashtag to continue the conversation. And yes, offering pizza or other food options is perfectly fine.

Impact: This event blends a popular food choice with valuable teachings, making it enjoyable and enriching. The relaxed setting fosters deep conversations and learning.

The Scoop

Description: Hold an ice cream social with a twist—a Q&A session or teaching segment. Serve a variety of ice cream flavors and offer a platform for questions or discussions. Ice cream is a great icebreaker, and the relaxed setting can encourage participation in the Q&A.

Why It's Easy: Ice cream socials are easy to set up and can be held indoors or outdoors. The Q&A or teaching segment can be informal and engaging. If you're familiar with our "Do We Know You?" exercise, you know that securing ice cream sponsorship could be easy if you have strong relationships with key stores in your city.

Impact: This event is a fun and interactive way to engage with the youth while enjoying a sweet treat. Combining ice cream and learning makes for a memorable and enjoyable experience.

P3 aka Praise, Preaching, and Prizes

Description: Organize an event featuring praise music, a preaching session, and prize giveaways. Include interactive elements like games or raffles to keep the energy high. This event combines praise music, a message of encouragement, and exciting prize giveaways. It can be as simple as setting up a sound system and inviting local musicians to lead worship. Prizes add an element of excitement and can be used as incentives for attendance or participation. Follow up by inviting attendees to regular worship services or special events.

Why It's Easy: This event requires basic planning, focusing on music, a speaker, and some prizes. It can be hosted almost anywhere—a park, fun park, outside a local pizza spot, cof-

Creativity

fee bar, football field, church parking lot, or neighborhood clubhouse.

The energy and excitement of prizes add an extra layer of fun. Get your *"Do We Know You?"* reputation up (more on this later) because if P3 strikes a chord in your city, you'll need a lot of prizes!

Impact: This event provides a mix of worship, spiritual growth, and excitement through prizes. It's engaging and encourages participation, setting the stage for a positive and energetic atmosphere.

Gospel Grill

Description:

1. Host a barbecue or grilling event with gospel music and fellowship.

2. Set up a grill, serve great food, and play uplifting gospel tunes.

3. Plan to connect with attendees after the event through small groups or community service projects, as this event is particularly effective for reaching college students and young adults.

Why It's Easy: Grilling events are easy to organize with minimal equipment—just a grill, food, and music (DJ). It combines good food with a joyful atmosphere.

Impact: The Gospel Grill is more than just an event—it's a powerful opportunity to connect with others and share the love of Christ. We recently hosted a Gospel Grill with my USC Upstate students, which was truly transformative. The atmosphere was filled with laughter, conversation, and uplifting gospel music. Most importantly, three students decided to accept Christ as their Savior. This casual, fun gathering encouraged socializing and community building, demonstrating the profound impact that such a simple event can have.

WHAT WILL YOU DO?

When you have their attention, what will you do with it?

A fall festival without Christian education is nothing more than a circus; a cookout without content is just a mere drop-in. Students need to hear the Word of God every chance they get! We should be utterly obsessed with being equipped to teach the Word of God with grace, accuracy, and creativity so that students walk away with the Word deeply embedded in their hearts. If we truly believe that Christ is the way, God is the Creator, and the Holy Ghost is our guide, we must desire for the next generation to experience all God has for them through our teaching.

A scripture in Deuteronomy calls us to preserve the Word of God, saying, "Fix these words of mine in your hearts and minds; tie them as symbols on your hands and bind them on your foreheads" (Deuteronomy 11:18).

Revelation is powerful. We are sharing truths that have the power to pull a student out of depression, suicide pacts, and addictions.

Romans 2:15 tells us that God has written moral truths on the tablets of our hearts: "They show that the requirements of the law are written on their hearts, their consciences also bearing witness." But in this noisy, anti-Christ society, it's all too easy to suppress that truth.

Creativity

Teacher, you matter. Gone are the days of simply handing out a cute little game to pass the time until "Big Church" is over.

The quality of your teaching for the next generation will directly affect the quality of your future caregivers, politicians, doctors, law enforcers, and so on. You are helping shape the worldview of young minds.

We will delve deeper into the importance of helping students understand why they believe what they believe and how to defend their faith in the "Contend in the Culture" chapter.

However, let's focus on how we can make the content stick.

How can we help the light bulb come on for kids who are below our shoulders and still wet cement?

How can we mold their minds and hearts to be set on the Word of God, know it, live it, and share it?

This work is our calling, and it is a noble one. Let's rise to it with passion and purpose. Parables, like teaching, are tools to help the content stick.

Don't sleep on Jesus—He's the master teacher. Sometimes, we mistake His parables for simple, easy-to-understand stories, but Jesus taught in parables to conceal meaning. His teachings were used to hide the truth from those not open to receiving it. In Matthew 13:10-15, Jesus explains to His disciples that He uses parables because many people are unwilling to see, hear, or understand the truth due to their hardened hearts.

That verse almost made me hesitant to promote parables

as a teaching model because don't we want youth to understand?

Of course, we do!

When you look at parables, you can see many benefits to the framework. Youth are naturally thinkers and inquisitive. Many students will want to solve a riddle, especially if they know an incentive is waiting for them if they get it right.

Parables can be an excellent model for teaching youth because they are engaging, relatable, and effective in conveying complex ideas in a way that encourages understanding and reflection.

Here's why parables are particularly suitable for Christian education:

1. **Relatable Stories:** Parables use everyday situations and familiar elements, making them relatable to young people. Parables connect spiritual lessons to things they encounter daily, so they help youth understand and internalize important teachings.

2. **Engagement Through Storytelling:** Youth are naturally drawn to stories, which makes parables an effective way to capture their attention. The narrative structure of parables keeps young listeners engaged and interested, making it easier for them to remember and apply the lessons.

3. **Encourages Critical Thinking:** Parables often contain layers of meaning and symbolism that require thought and reflection. Likewise, they challenge youth to think critically, explore deeper truths, and grow personally.

4. **Provokes Curiosity and Discussion:** The open-

ended nature of many parables invites questions and discussions, providing opportunities for youth to express their thoughts and engage with others. This dialogue helps reinforce understanding and allows youth to explore different perspectives.

5. **Moral and Ethical Lessons:** Parables often convey moral and ethical lessons relevant to young people's lives. They provide biblical guidance on values, behavior, and relationships, helping youth navigate complex social and personal situations.

6. **Memorable and Impactful:** The use of vivid imagery and memorable characters makes parables stick in the minds of young people. The stories are easy to recall, which helps reinforce the lessons over time.

7. **Encourages Empathy and Understanding:** Parables often explore compassion, forgiveness, and justice themes. By identifying with characters and situations in the stories, youth can develop empathy and a deeper understanding of these important virtues.

8. **Adaptable to Modern Contexts:** The timeless nature of parables allows them to be adapted to modern contexts, making them relevant to today's youth. Educators can use contemporary examples to illustrate similar lessons and make the teachings more applicable.

By incorporating the parables into youth education, teachers and mentors can create an engaging and effective learning environment that encourages young people to think deeply, explore their faith, and develop valuable life skills.

Here's a quick "parable cheat sheet." We provided two in case one resonates better than the other.

Personally, I prefer the STORY framework.

STORY FRAMEWORK

- **S:** Select Core Message - Identify the key lesson or principle you want to convey.
- **T:** Themes Relatable - Choose familiar, everyday elements that resonate with the audience.
- **O:** Outline Narrative - Develop a compelling and engaging story with characters and a plot.
- **R:** Relate Symbolism - Use symbols and metaphors to convey deeper meanings.
- **Y:** Yield Reflection - Encourage discussion and personal application of the lesson.

STORY FRAMEWORK EXAMPLE

Bottom Line: Don't be so quick to overreact.

S: Select Core Message

The core message emphasizes the importance of pausing and thinking before reacting, especially when emotions run high.

T: Themes Relatable

Use familiar scenarios that youth can relate to, such as conflicts with friends, social media arguments, or family disagreements.

O: Outline Narrative

Story Title: "The Instant Reply"

Plot:

Creativity

- **Characters:** Alex, Jamie, and a group of friends
- **Setting:** A high school environment
- **Conflict:** Jamie posts a comment on social media that Alex finds offensive. Alex feels a surge of anger and is about to respond impulsively.
- **Resolution:** Alex's friend notices his reaction and advises him to take a moment to cool down. Alex steps away from his phone, reflects on the situation, and responds calmly and constructively. This leads to a resolution of the misunderstanding and improved communication.

R: Relate Symbolism

Symbolism:

- **Phone Notifications:** Represent the immediate urge to react.
- **Timer/Clock:** Symbolizes taking time to reflect before responding.
- **Cool-Down Space:** A physical space where Alex goes to calm down, representing the mental pause needed before reacting.

Y: Yield Reflection

Questions to Encourage Discussion:

- "Have you ever reacted quickly to something that you later regretted? How did it turn out?"

- "What ways can you pause and reflect before reacting in a heated situation?"

- "How can taking a moment to cool down improve your relationships with others?"

This framework provides a modern-day example that

illustrates the importance of pausing and reflecting before reacting, helping youth understand and apply the lesson in their lives.

This story underscores the importance of listening and reflecting before speaking or reacting, reinforcing the core message of not being quick to "pop off." It ties the story and lesson together by emphasizing patience and thoughtful response.

PARABLE FRAMEWORK

- **P: Pick Core Message** - Determine the main lesson or principle.

- **A: Add Relatable Themes** - Use familiar elements to make the story relatable.

- **R: Render a Story** - Create an engaging narrative with a clear plot and characters.

- **A: Apply Symbolism** - Incorporate symbols and metaphors for deeper insights.

- **B: Build Reflection** - Promote discussion and personal reflection on the story.

- **L: Link to Modern Contexts** - Relate the parable to contemporary issues and experiences.

- **E: Ensure Application** - Provide practical steps for applying the lesson in real life.

M3 TEACHING BLUEPRINT

For over 20 years, I have combined three modalities for Bi-

Creativity

ble teaching: **Music, Motion, and Motivation**.

Music: This can include a remix of a melody with relevant content, a rap, chant, music bed behind the content, instruments, or even poetry turned musical. Live music triggers melody. Consider this: When you eat a good meal, do you often sing and dance? What if the Word of God was attached to that melody? Everything can be musical—listen for syllables, rhythm, and pitch.

Motion: Incorporate motion with the content. Think about how you can turn any word into a motion. View words as living, breathing beings that inspire you to move. Add simple gestures, dances, or full choreography; even standing up, sitting down, walking, running, or clapping counts as motion. When you clap, you combine motion and music into one.

Motivation: Motivation is key to maintaining classroom control, order, and discipline. Motivation can be based on competition. Consider how you can make everything competitive, encouraging students to compete with themselves, each other, or even you as the teacher. Examples include competitions to see who can speak the loudest, fastest, or slowest. Please encourage students to be their best and reward behaviors you want to promote with compliments, handclaps, thumbs-ups, pats on the back, and high-fives.

Motivation boosts morale and can include incentives to encourage participation. Although I am naturally musical, motivation is one of my favorite techniques because it transforms everything into a game. Teaching using games makes you a more effective teacher and helps the content stick.

The M3 Teaching Blueprint can be a game-changer and lifesaver in last-minute situations. One of the favorite parts of our live training sessions is the challenge where you teach using one of these three elements to different age groups. Imagine walking into church, and your pastor, Christian Ed director, or youth pastor says, "We need you to fill in this morning to teach."

You are only given a Bible verse or a theme. They may even say, "Teach whatever you want."

What will you do?

Pull out the M3 Teaching Framework!

Examples of M3 in Action:

Music:

- **Elementary School**: Use a catchy song to help young children memorize Bible verses or historical facts.
- **Middle School**: Create a rap or song about a scientific concept to engage students in a fun way.
- **High School**: Incorporate popular music themes to discuss social issues and encourage critical thinking.

Motion:

- **Elementary School**: Use dance or simple movements to explain math concepts or storytelling.
- **Middle School**: Organize a scavenger hunt that requires physical activity and problem-solving skills.
- **High School**: Develop a role-play activity where students act out historical events to understand the context and impact better.

Motivation (Competition and Games):

- **Elementary School**: Use a "Question of the

Day" challenge, where students compete to see who can answer best. Offer instant rewards, like stickers or extra recess time, to motivate participation and good behavior.

- **Middle School**: Implement a classroom leaderboard where students earn points for answering questions correctly and demonstrating good behavior. At the end of each day, the top scorers can choose a small privilege, like selecting the next classroom activity.

- **High School**: Facilitate a "Lightning Round" quiz at the end of each lesson, where students compete to answer as many questions as possible within a set time. Offer immediate feedback and bonus points toward their final grade to encourage focus and enthusiasm.

These strategies aim to motivate students through immediate incentives, enhancing engagement and learning while promoting positive behavior.

If you want your teacher to be coached, consider our teaching certification cohort, where we dig deep into the M3 Teaching Blueprint and how to teach using technology.

OUTSOURCING CREATIVITY IN TEACHING

In today's dynamic learning environment, it's perfectly okay to outsource creativity when needed. As educators, it's important to recognize that we don't have to excel in every area ourselves. Sometimes, external expertise can significantly enhance the learning experience and deliver messages more effectively.

For example, if delivering engaging and impactful lessons isn't your strong suit, consider outsourcing to a live presenter whose genius lies in captivating audiences. This approach lets you focus on your strengths while ensuring students receive high-quality, engaging instruction.

However, it's essential to establish clear parameters when outsourcing creativity. Ensure that the person or resource aligns with your educational goals and values, maintaining consistency with the messages you wish to convey. By setting these boundaries, you can leverage external creativity while staying true to the core mission of your teaching.

Outsourcing doesn't diminish your role but enhances your ability to provide a comprehensive and enriching learning experience. Embrace the opportunity to collaborate with creative experts and use their talents to inspire and engage your students, ultimately achieving your educational objectives.

BENEFITS OF USING SCREENS AND TEACHING VIDEOS

Incorporating screens and teaching videos from platforms like YouTube or purchased pre-recorded materials can significantly enhance the learning experience in your teaching environment. Here are some key benefits:

1. **Engagement and Interest**: Screens and videos capture students' attention more effectively than traditional methods. Visual and auditory elements can bring lessons to life, making complex concepts easier to understand and remember.

2. **Accessibility and Variety**: With a vast array of videos available, educators can choose content that fits their au-

Creativity

dience's specific needs and interests. This variety can cater to different learning styles—visual, auditory, or kinesthetic—ensuring that all students are engaged.

3. **Consistency and Quality**: Using pre-recorded content ensures that the quality and delivery of the information are consistent every time. This method can be especially beneficial for teaching complex topics or when the educator wants to ensure that a specific message is communicated clearly.

4. **Flexibility and Convenience**: Screens and videos allow educators to integrate diverse materials seamlessly into their lesson plans. They can be used to introduce topics, reinforce learning, or provide real-world examples that relate directly to the subject matter.

5. **Focus and Alignment with Goals**: It is crucial to ensure that the content aligns with the desired outcomes and the spiritual guidance you wish to convey. Rather than taking a random approach, educators should select videos and materials that support what God is speaking to them about and align with the bottom line they desire for their students. This purposeful selection ensures that the content reinforces the values and messages they aim to impart.

6. **Interactive and Collaborative Learning**: Screens can facilitate interactive learning experiences, such as live polls or group discussions based on video content. This interaction can create a collaborative learning environment where students actively participate and engage with the material.

7. **Inspiration and Motivation**: High-quality videos often feature inspiring stories, expert insights, or dynamic pre-

sentations that can motivate students and spark their curiosity. This inspiration can lead to a deeper understanding and a stronger connection to the subject matter.

Using screens and teaching videos can be a powerful tool in education, provided the content is chosen with intention and aligns with the teaching program's overarching goals and spiritual direction. By doing so, educators can create a dynamic and impactful learning environment that resonates with their students on multiple levels.

DO YOU CODE SWITCH?

In a social context, code-switching is changing how you talk to fit in with different people or situations. It means switching up your language, slang, or how you speak based on who you're with or where you are. Whether moving between languages or switching from your chill talk with friends to a more polished vibe with adults or at work, it's all about adapting your style to match the scene.

Certainly! Here are examples of how you might teach Philippians 4:13 ("I can do all things through Christ who strengthens me") to different age groups, with each delivery tailored to their developmental stage and interests:

Children (Ages 6-10)

Teaching Method: Interactive Storytelling with Visual Aids

Example:

1. Start with a story about a young superhero who faces a challenge but succeeds with the help of their special powers.

Creativity

2. Show colorful images or a short, animated video of the superhero overcoming obstacles with Christ's strength.

3. Use simple, relatable language to explain how the superhero's strength is like the strength we get from Christ to handle our challenges.

Engagement: Ask the children to draw or act out a time when they felt strong or overcame something difficult and relate it to how Christ helps us in those moments.

Teenagers (Ages 13-18)

Teaching Method: Group Discussion and Real-life Applications

Example:

1. Discuss real-life scenarios teens face, like exams, sports, or personal struggles.

2. Share personal stories or testimonies from young adults who have relied on their faith to overcome challenges.

3. Use a discussion format to explore how Philippians 4:13 can apply to their experiences and encourage them to think about specific situations where they need strength.

Engagement: Use multimedia resources such as video clips from influencers or athletes discussing faith and perseverance. Facilitate group discussions or role-playing exercises to help them relate the verse to their daily lives.

Young Adults (Ages 18-25)

Teaching Method: Interactive Workshops and Goal-Setting

Exercises

Example:

1. Start with a workshop focused on personal and professional goals.

2. Discuss how Philippians 4:13 can be a source of motivation and resilience in pursuing these goals.

3. Use case studies or interviews with professionals who have faced significant obstacles and relied on their faith for strength.

Engagement: Encourage participants to set personal goals or tackle challenges they are facing. Have them write down their goals and how they plan to rely on Christ's strength to achieve them. Incorporate prayer or meditation sessions to reflect on the verse's impact on their ambitions.

General Teaching Tips Across Ages

1. **Relatable Analogies:** Tailor analogies and examples to the age group's experiences and interests. For younger children, use simple, visual stories; for teens and young adults, incorporate real-world scenarios and practical applications.

2. **Interactive Elements:** Engage the audience with activities appropriate to their age. Hands-on activities, discussions, or digital media can make the verse more meaningful.

3. **Encouragement and Support:** Ensure each age group feels supported and encouraged. Emphasize that relying on Christ's strength empowers them for all challenges they face.

Creativity

Adapting your delivery to fit each age group's developmental stage and interests makes Philippians 4:13 more relatable and impactful for your audience.

When it comes to creativity, what better place to express it than in music? We want to offer a streamlined version of our Youth Choir framework, which has worked for over twenty years and continues to thrive today. Youth choirs have been a staple in many of our churches. Before elaborate children's church programs, the youth choir served as a hub for community, fellowship, and Christian education and a training ground for the next generation of youth leaders.

Traditionally, youth choirs were cool places for kids to sing and showcase their talent, especially for kids like my siblings and me. While some kids chose sports, many were drawn to music. However, somewhere along the way, the youth choir began to decline. With more options available in churches, like dance and step teams, parents no longer mandated participation in youth choirs.

Over the years, we have witnessed youth choirs diminish and even disappear in our region, all while our youth choir, Pure-N-Heart, flourishes. One reason for our success is that kids who love to sing need a place to belong. Once those children stepped foot in a Pure-N-Heart rehearsal, they were hooked. They found a place to sing cool music, meet new friends, learn about God, worship, and have fun.

We've even seen students skip soccer practice to attend our youth choir rehearsals. They chose our choir over other extracurricular activities because we didn't just have rehearsals or workshops; we created EVENTS. That's the key. Make every rehearsal an EVENT, and you'll see an increase in retention in your youth choir. By transforming rehearsals into engaging and dynamic experiences, you create an environment where young people are excited to participate and grow.

Our framework for reviving or starting a youth choir is found in the acronym E.V.E.N.T.

E.V.E.N.T.

E: Energetic Rehearsals

- Conduct lively and dynamic rehearsals that energize participants.
- Incorporate elements of a service, such as praise, prayer, and worship songs, to create a meaningful flow.
- Use interactive activities to maintain enthusiasm and focus.

V: Visionary Goals

- Set clear and inspiring goals for the choir, including upcoming performances.
- Develop a comprehensive plan for engaging parents and keeping them informed and involved.
- Establish a timeline for achieving milestones and preparing for concerts.

E: Engaging Rewards

- Provide engaging incentives to encourage participation and dedication.
- Use rewards like special recognition, leadership

Creativity

roles, or fun outings to motivate choir members.

- Recognize achievements and progress to connect youth to an accomplishment.

N: Nurturing Atmosphere

- Create a nurturing environment where everyone feels welcome and valued.
- Offer snacks after rehearsals to encourage fellowship and connection among members.
- Organize community-building activities that strengthen relationships and unity.

T: Transformative Leadership

- Appoint a dedicated director who is passionate about the choir's mission.
- Ensure the director is committed to excellence and inspires the choir to reach its full potential.
- Support the director with resources and training to enhance their leadership skills.

This version maintains the core ideas while providing a fresh take on the essential elements for starting a successful youth choir.

EVENT STRATEGIES

Are you ready to take your event promotion to the next level?

Think about creating a buzz that draws people in and gets them talking long after the event is over.

Here are some innovative marketing and promotion ideas for your children's church, youth event, worship night, block party, and back-to-school bash. These strategies include non-traditional approaches, unique partnerships, and engaging tactics to ensure your event succeeds!

Why not start by renting a bounce house and featuring it prominently in your promotions? Instead of saving the best elements for the day of the event, use them in your marketing to give attendees a sneak peek of the excitement. It's like offering a free sample of ice cream or cookies—once they get a taste, they'll be eager for more. Consider taking over an existing service with elements of what's to come or cross-promote with other events to expand your reach and excitement.

By weaving these creative ideas into your promotional strategy, you'll create an irresistible pull with everyone marking their calendars and spreading the word.

Don't forget the T.Y.M approach (we will share more on this in the chapter on "Community and Collaboration"), which will take some pressure off.

GENERAL MARKETING AND PROMOTION STRATEGIES

Social Media Challenges

Strategy: Launch a series of challenges on platforms like TikTok or Instagram, where participants complete fun tasks related to the event theme (e.g., posting their best worship dance moves or creating art inspired by the event).

Promotion: Encourage participants to tag friends and use a

Creativity

unique event hashtag to spread the challenge virally. Offer prizes for the most creative entries.

Interactive Storytelling Campaigns

Strategy: Develop a multi-part story on social media that unfolds over time, with each post or video revealing more about the event and its significance. Engage the audience by allowing them to vote on the direction of the story or submit their own contributions.

Promotion: Use platforms like Instagram Stories, Snapchat, or Facebook Live to create engaging and interactive narratives that build anticipation.

Collaborative Live Streams

Strategy: Partner with local influencers, youth leaders, or community figures to host live streams discussing the event, sharing personal stories, and answering questions.

Promotion: Use these sessions to offer sneak peeks, announce special guests, or reveal exclusive content. Promote the live streams across social media and through email newsletters.

Personalized Invitations

Strategy: Create personalized video invitations from key event figures, youth leaders, or influencers addressing the recipient by name and inviting them to the event.

Promotion: Distribute these invitations via email or social media direct messages, making recipients feel special and personally connected to the event.

Event Previews and Teasers

Strategy: Share short, engaging videos or posts that provide a glimpse into what attendees can expect at the event, such as highlights from previous events, behind-the-scenes footage, or interviews with performers.

Promotion: Use these teasers to create excitement and anticipation and encourage sharing with friends and family.

Community Service Tie-Ins

Strategy: Organize a community service project leading up to the event, inviting youth and parents to participate and promoting the event to celebrate their contributions.

Promotion: Partner with local charities or community organizations to amplify the message and reach a broader audience. Share stories and images of the service project on social media.

Pop-Up Worship Experience

Concept: Host a series of surprise pop-up worship sessions in unexpected locations like parks, malls, or urban areas, featuring live music and youth speakers. Think of other areas in your city for these experiences. Every region has unique venues and areas great for this.

Promotion: Collaborate with local influencers to announce each location just hours before it happens on social media, building excitement and urgency

Gospel Flash Mob

Concept: Organize a gospel flash mob at a popular location to create a buzz around the worship night.

Promotion: Record the flash mob and post it online with details of the worship night. Collaborate with local gospel choirs to participate and spread the word. A great deal of research will be needed to know who the choirs are, and a social media savvy person is critical to help manage the online posting.

Farm-to-Table Worship Picnic

Concept: Host a worship night at a local farm, combining worship with a farm-to-table picnic featuring local produce. This is a great idea for rural or country areas.

Promotion: Partner with local farmers and food vendors to provide fresh produce and meals. Use social media to share behind-the-scenes footage of meal preparations and farm life. This would likely go viral on your youth ministry YouTube channel.

Block Party in a Big City

1. Street Art Festival

Concept: Organize a street art festival where local artists create murals, installations, and performances inspired by the event's themes.

Promotion: Work with art schools or galleries to attract artists and enthusiasts. Use social media to live-stream art creations and artist interviews. This collaboration with schools will generate a ripple effect that fills up your event. Nothing like word of mouth.

2. Food Truck Rally and Worship

Concept: Bring together a variety of food trucks and set up stages for live worship performances in a city square or park.

Promotion: Collaborate with food truck vendors to offer special deals or dishes themed around the event. Use food bloggers and social media to promote the rally.

Back-to-School Event in the Country

Outdoor Adventure Day

Concept: Host an outdoor adventure day with activities like hiking, fishing, or obstacle courses paired with lessons on faith and resilience.

Promotion: Partner with local outdoor clubs or adventure companies to provide equipment and expertise. Use social media to create excitement with videos of nature and adventure tips.

Harvest Festival and Worship Night

Concept: Celebrate the start of the school year with a harvest festival, featuring local produce, crafts, and a worship service under the stars.

Promotion: Work with local farmers and artisans to provide goods and crafts. Use social media to share stories of the local community and the significance of harvest time. Even though we think it would work well in the mountains or foothills this concept should be interesting in other areas.

Planning and Social Media Strategy

1. Countdown Campaigns

Use a countdown campaign on social media leading up to the event, with daily teasers, testimonials, or behind-the-scenes content to maintain engagement.

2. Influencer Partnerships

Collaborate with local influencers, youth leaders, or popular community figures to promote the events through their platforms.

Creativity

3. Event Hashtag Challenge

Create a unique hashtag for each event and encourage attendees to share their excitement, stories, or creative interpretations of the theme.

4. Collaborative Playlists

Invite participants to contribute to a Spotify playlist for the event, featuring songs that inspire and energize them.

5. Video Invitations

Create personalized video invitations from key event figures or youth leaders to send to targeted groups or individuals.

Combining these creative ideas with strategic planning and collaboration allows you to create memorable events that resonate with your target audience and drive attendance.

Runway to Success

1. Event Countdown with Daily Activities

Strategy: Create a countdown calendar with daily activities or tasks related to the event, such as trivia questions, challenges, or community engagement opportunities.

Promotion: Share these activities on social media and encourage followers to participate and share their experiences, building momentum leading up to the event.

2. Influencer Takeovers

Strategy: Arrange for local influencers or youth leaders to "take over" your social media accounts for a day, sharing their thoughts, experiences, and excitement about the event.

Promotion: Use this opportunity to reach the influencer's audience and provide a fresh perspective on the event's appeal.

3. Community Art Installation

Strategy: Commission a local artist to create a temporary art installation in a prominent location inspired by the event's theme.

Promotion: Use the installation as a photo opportunity and social media focal point, encouraging attendees to visit, take photos, and share their experiences online.

By implementing these creative marketing and promotion strategies, you can effectively engage youth and their parents, generate excitement, and increase attendance at your events.

SOCIAL MEDIA

Navigating social media in youth ministry offers significant benefits, such as increased outreach and community building, but also presents challenges. Here are three advantages with outcomes and three drawbacks with strategies to mitigate them, ensuring a balanced approach.

Advantages:

1. Increased Outreach and Participation

Outcome: Social media enables the ministry to reach large numbers of youth, including those who might not attend church regularly. This broader outreach can increase participation in ministry events and activities, building a vibrant and active youth group.

2. Enhanced Communication and Engagement

Outcome: Effective use of social media can lead to better communication and engagement with the youth. Timely updates, inspirational posts, and interactive content can keep the youth interested and involved, resulting in a more connected and engaged community.

3. Strengthened Sense of Community

Outcome: Social media can help build a sense of community among the youth by providing a platform for continuous interaction. This ongoing connection can lead to stronger relationships, support networks, and a deeper sense of belonging within the ministry.

Drawbacks:

1. Increased Digital Distraction

Outcome: Social media's pervasive nature can lead to youth becoming more distracted and less focused on spiritual growth and face-to-face interactions. This can result in superficial engagement with the ministry and hinder deeper, more meaningful connections.

Mitigation: Establish clear guidelines for social media use within the ministry, such as designated times for online engagement and periods of digital detox. Encourage youth to balance their online activities with offline spiritual practices, like regular prayer and Bible study, to maintain focus on their faith journey.

2. Exposure to Negative Influences

Outcome: Youth are at risk of encountering cyberbullying, harmful content, and negative influences on social media. This exposure can lead to emotional distress, decreased self-esteem, and a potential deviation from positive ministry messages and values.

Mitigation: Create a Safe Online Environment - Monitor social media interactions within the ministry and promote positive, uplifting content. Educate youth about recognizing and responding to cyberbullying and negative influences. Create a supportive community where youth feel comfortable reporting any concerning online behavior, ensuring timely intervention and support.

3. Privacy and Security Risks

Outcome: The challenge of maintaining privacy on social media can lead to the unintended sharing of personal information and photos, resulting in privacy breaches. Privacy breaches cause discomfort and mistrust among the youth and their families, potentially damaging the ministry's reputation and relationships.

Mitigation: Educate on Privacy Best Practices - Conduct regular workshops or sessions on online privacy and security. Teach youth how to protect their personal information, use privacy settings effectively, and understand the implications of sharing content online. Establish and enforce privacy protocols within the ministry's social media platforms to safeguard personal data and build trust among youth and their families. *Alexias is a cybersecurity professional, and we cannot stress this enough. A best practice is to host regular security sessions with the youth and the entire church community.*

Focusing on these outcomes emphasizes the impact social media can have on the youth ministry and highlights the potential benefits and challenges that need to be managed.

Creativity

THE CASE FOR A YOUTUBE CHANNEL

A YouTube channel is essential for youth ministries as it provides a dynamic platform to reach and engage young people who already spend considerable time watching videos.

YouTube is the most popular social media platform among the 12-21 age group, with 93% of U.S. adults aged 18-29 using it and users spending an average of 48.7 minutes daily on the platform. This trend also extends to younger teens.

Video content allows for creative expression of faith, sharing of testimonies, and disseminating inspirational messages in an easily accessible format. It enhances community building by offering a space for interactive content like live Q&A sessions, virtual Bible studies, and event recaps.

Moreover, YouTube's vast reach can attract new members and provide a sense of connection for those unable to attend in person.

Source: Statista

Social media app usage among Generation Z in the United States

Today, social media apps are utilized by Gen Z (users who are aged between 16 to 25 years old) at a large scale. According to Statista, 92% of Gen Z users in the U.S. access YouTube the most. Followed by Instagram in the second position with 85% of the share of users, and TikTok in the third position with 78% of Gen Z users.

Below we have mentioned a table showcasing social media app usage according to Gen Z in the United States:

Social Media App	Share of users
YouTube	92%
Instagram	85%
TikTok	78%
Discord	42%

Table 3. Social Media App Usage

Social media offers an incredible opportunity for youth ministries to connect with young people where they are, sharing messages of faith and community in engaging ways. A YouTube channel can amplify this reach, providing dynamic, accessible content that inspires spiritual growth and builds a supportive community.

9
COMMUNITY AND COLLABORATION

The day we turned a tragic event into an opportunity to unify the church, the community, and our government. And guess what? The youth led the way!

Impact events—those events that are ingrained in your memory forever. You may not remember the specifics of your day last Tuesday or even the Tuesday before. Still, many recall exactly where they were and what they were doing on Tuesday, September 11, 2001, when they heard the news of the catastrophic events that day. One of us was in a statistics class, the other in a religion class. We still remember it nearly twenty-five years later.

That "impact event" changed the lives of many families and loved ones, changing the trajectory of security in the U.S. and the world.

We were never the same.

June 2015 had a similar impact on us. Imagine coming together for Bible Study. It was just like any other Wednesday, except this night, there was a guest. An unknown young man sat with the small congregation in the historic Mother Emanuel AME Church for an hour before opening fire, killing nine parishioners, including the pastor and South Carolina senator, Reverend Clementa Pinckney—a husband and father. Being from South Carolina and having visited Charleston our entire lives, these events shook us to our core.

Later, we discovered that the young man (we refuse to acknowledge him by name) aimed to start a race war by needlessly murdering these fathers, mothers, sons, and daughters. But it didn't work!

Using our influence with churches, parents, and youth, we were inspired to host one of the most significant events of its kind in Greenville, SC—a "Saving Our Youth" community event.

This was our first massive TYM (Tandem Youth Ministry) experience. So, what is TYM? Tandem Youth Ministry is an intentional, collaborative approach where youth ministries and leaders work together to promote the Gospel of Jesus Christ. These ministries coordinate efforts, share resources and funding, and support one another. The outcome is more significant than any one ministry can achieve on its own.

For Saving Our Youth, we stepped outside the traditional church network. We included community organizations such as a local orchestra, a dance coalition, top talent in the city, and government officials. Our mayor was present, along with many state and local representatives. We also rented the Greenville Drive minor league baseball stadium. It was a sight to behold. Thousands attended and participated—an undertaking only possible with the joint efforts and support of hundreds of leaders.

Community and Collaboration

The guests of honor?

We honored a local pastor, Pastor Curtis Johnson, who has spent his life making a difference in our community, as well as the survivors of the Charleston 9 shooting. Many do not know that not everyone in the church lost their lives that day. We honored them with love and intention. And the real treat—Reverend Pinckney's daughters sang with our youth choir, Pure-N-Heart. It was our way to amplify the preached Word by Pastor Sean Dogan, who shared a message of unity and resilience and the melodious Gospel of our Savior in the streets of downtown Greenville, SC. Pastor Dogan, a generous and prominent pastor in our region, reminded our common enemy that we would not be subject to his devices: "As for you, you meant evil against me, but God meant it for good in order to bring about this present result, to keep many people alive." (Genesis 50:20).

WAYS TO USE TANDEM YOUTH MINISTRY (TYM)

1. Joint Events and Retreats

Example: Three local churches collaborate to host an annual weekend retreat focused on spiritual growth and team-building activities. By pooling their resources, they can invite a well-known speaker and provide various workshops.

Outcome: Youth from different churches form lasting friendships, gain a deeper understanding of their faith, and feel a stronger sense of community and support. Increased participation in future church activities is observed.

Benefits: Economies of scale reduce costs for each church; exposure to diverse perspectives and teachings enriches the youth's spiritual journey; large-scale events create excitement and draw higher attendance.

2. Shared Resources and Programs

Example: Two churches create a shared mentorship program where older youth mentor younger peers from both congregations. They also established a joint Bible study group that meets weekly, rotating between the churches' facilities.

Outcome: Mentorship relationships flourish, leading to improved leadership skills and spiritual growth among the older youth. The Bible study group builds connections with increased engagement in discipleship activities.

Benefits: Resource sharing maximizes the impact without duplicating efforts; younger youth receive guidance and support from more experienced peers; the rotational meetings build camaraderie across the churches.

3. Leader Exchange and Training:

Example: Four churches organize a leader exchange program where youth leaders from each church take turns leading youth group sessions at the other churches. Additionally, they host quarterly training workshops on topics like conflict resolution, creative teaching methods, and effective discipleship strategies.

Outcome: Youth leaders gain new perspectives and techniques, enhancing their effectiveness in ministry. The shared training workshops lead to a more skilled and confident leadership team, resulting in more dynamic and impactful youth programs across all participating churches.

Benefits: Leaders gain fresh insights and avoid burnout through new experiences; shared training resources increase the quality of leadership development; consistent training ensures all leaders are aligned in their approach, creating a more unified and effective ministry.

TYM is only as great as the relationships that sustain it. A friend always says, "Life moves at the speed of relationships."

Pause momentarily and assess what we can accomplish if we try TYM tomorrow.

MARKET RESEARCH

Welcome to a working session. Grab your tablet, computer, phone, journal, or even a scratch sheet of paper to capture your responses to the questions throughout this section on market research. The exercise is worthwhile and can transform your youth ministry if used strategically, as market research allows us to dig deeper to understand environmental factors that could impact our success.

Below is a fill-in-the-blank exercise that allows you to examine the potential for youth ministries, after-school programs, or community organizations.

How many neighborhoods, supermarkets, community centers, sports complexes, schools, and apartment buildings are near your church or organization?

Knowing this information is invaluable.

Gathering this information will be helpful when planning and promoting youth events. The data will reveal food sponsors and other community partners who can support your efforts. Having solid relationships with these entities will be key to your success.

NO YOUTH, NO CHURCH SOULUTIONS

For this "Do We Know You?" exercise, take time to name at least five elements for each factor:

- Name five of the nearest apartment complexes.
- Name the five nearest sports complexes and parks (e.g., baseball field, soccer field, YMCA).
- Name five of the nearest community centers.
- Name five of the nearest elementary, middle, and high schools.
- Name five local restaurants.
- Name five of the nearest churches.
- Name five of the nearest neighborhood communities.
- Name five local supermarkets.
- Name five of the nearest food chains or pantries.
- Name five malls.
- Name five family parks within the city.
- Name the nearest flea market.
- Name five local pawn shops.
- Name at least five of the nearest colleges and universities.
- Name five local banks.

All these entities are asking, "Do we know you? Should we know you?" Engaging in the exercise will highlight your blind spots and list partners you may have overlooked. Consider adding to your directory for partnerships, sponsorships, and relationship building. The generated list will serve you well as you empower youth.

CHURCH COLLABORATION

Collaborating with other churches to host a youth event offers many benefits beyond any single congregation's reach. By joining forces, churches can significantly increase their reach and attendance, ensuring that more youth from diverse backgrounds are engaged.

This partnership allows for sharing resources, such as finances, volunteers, and equipment, leading to a more efficiently organized and high-quality event. Enhanced programming becomes possible with various activities and the attraction of notable speakers and performers, making the event more appealing and impactful. Additionally, such collaboration builds unity among churches, strengthens community bonds, and creates lasting relationships. The combined effort also results in greater logistical efficiency and innovation, as well as increased community recognition and support. By working together, churches can create a more profound and lasting impact on their youth and the broader community.

MAXIMIZING STRENGTHS THROUGH COLLABORATION

Each church can contribute its unique strengths to create a truly exceptional event in such a collaboration. For example, one church may have an ideal location with ample space, including a gymnasium perfect for hosting activities and sports. Another church may have a dedicated and large volunteer base, providing the necessary manpower to manage and execute various aspects of the event efficiently. A third church might possess the financial resources to fund the event, covering costs for equipment, guest speakers, and promotional materials.

Combining Resources

Venue and Facilities: The church, with the spacious gym, can offer its location as the primary venue, ensuring enough room for all planned activities and events.

Volunteers and Manpower: The church, with a strong volunteer network, can supply the necessary personnel to handle logistics, coordinate activities, and ensure smooth operations throughout the event.

Financial Support: The church, with substantial financial resources, can cover the costs of high-quality equipment, professional speakers, and marketing efforts, enhancing the overall quality and appeal of the event.

ADDITIONAL BENEFITS OF TYM

Enhanced Programming

Diverse Activities: Collaboration can bring together various ideas and activities, making the event more engaging and appealing to a broader range of interests.

Quality Speakers and Performers: Pooling resources can attract higher-profile speakers and performers who can draw more attendees and provide valuable content.

Stronger Community Bonds

Unity Among Churches: Working together builds an appreciation of unity and cooperation among different congregations, promoting shared purpose and mission.

Networking Opportunities: Creates opportunities for youth and leaders to network, build relationships, and promote belonging within the larger faith community.

Greater Impact

Spiritual Growth: A larger, well-attended event can have a significant spiritual impact, reaching more youth with the Gospel and planting and watering seeds for God to increase.

Long-Term Collaboration: Successful collaboration can pave the way for future joint initiatives, creating a sustained impact on the community.

Logistical Efficiency

Event Planning: Combining planning efforts can lead to more efficient use of time and resources, leveraging each church's organizational strengths.

Marketing and Promotion: Joint promotion can lead to a more extensive and effective marketing campaign, reaching more people through combined channels.

Innovation and Creativity

New Ideas: Collaboration encourages sharing new ideas and creative approaches, leading to a more dynamic and exciting event.

Learning Opportunities: Churches can learn from each other's experiences and best practices, improving their future events and initiatives.

Community Recognition and Support

Visibility: A more prominent, collaborative event can attract media attention and recognition from the wider community, highlighting the positive role of churches in local society.

Support and Sponsorship: Greater visibility and impact can attract support and sponsorship from local businesses and organizations, further enhancing the event.

By laying out these benefits methodically, churches can see the tangible and intangible advantages of collaboration, making it an attractive option for hosting impactful youth events.

Cultivating a strong reputation with various community entities such as grocery stores, banks, city officials, and recreational facilities is crucial for churches. These relationships can significantly enhance the church's ability to serve its congregation and the broader community. By developing these connections, churches can secure support, resources, and opportunities that enrich their programs and outreach efforts. Please reference the results of your market research.

BUILDING A POSITIVE REPUTATION

"A good name is to be chosen rather than great riches, and favor is better than silver or gold" (Proverbs 22:1).

1. **Resource Availability:** Establishing solid relationships with community entities ensures a steady flow of resources, from financial support to in-kind donations.

2. **Enhanced Outreach**: Collaborative efforts with local entities can extend the church's reach, allowing it to serve more people and address needs more broadly.

3. **Increased Credibility:** Positive relationships with respected community entities enhance the church's cred-

ibility and reputation.

4. **Mutual Support:** Churches can offer support to these entities in return, creating a network of mutual benefit and shared goals.

5. **Community Engagement:** Active partnerships encourage greater community involvement and engagement in church activities, promoting unity and shared purpose.

Have a positive reputation in your church and community before attempting to establish external partnerships. Focusing time on developing community relationships will yield many positive outcomes. The following is a sample.

THE IMPORTANCE OF CHURCH-COMMUNITY RELATIONSHIPS

Financial Institutions (Banks and Credit Unions)

Example: Establishing a relationship with a local bank can lead to sponsorships or grants for community programs.

Why: Banks often have community outreach initiatives and can provide financial education workshops, support for capital projects, or sponsorships for church events.

Grocery Stores and Supermarkets

Example: Partnering with a local grocery store can facilitate food drives and donations for community meals.

Why: These partnerships ensure a reliable food source for church-led initiatives such as food pantries, holiday meal distributions, and community events.

City Officials and Local Government

Example: Regular communication with city officials can help churches stay informed about local policies and opportunities for collaboration.

Why: Engaging with local government can lead to support for community development projects, access to public places for events, and participation in civic initiatives.

Parks and Recreation Departments

Example: Collaborating with the parks department to host outdoor events and recreational activities for youth.

Why: Public parks can enhance church events, provide safe places for gatherings, and promote community wellness through organized sports and activities.

Fun Parks and Entertainment Venues

Example: Partnering with local amusement parks for discounted group rates or special event days for church members.

Why: These partnerships can provide unique fellowship opportunities and enhance youth programs with fun and engaging outings.

Local Schools and Educational Institutions

Example: Working with schools to support after-school programs and tutoring services.

Why: Collaboration with educational institutions can enhance academic support for youth, provide venues for educational events, and create volunteer opportunities for church members.

Health and Wellness Centers

Example: Partnering with clinics and fitness centers to offer health screenings and wellness programs.

Why: These partnerships promote physical health and well-being within the congregation, providing valuable services such as free health check-ups and fitness classes.

Small Businesses and Local Shops

Example: Encouraging church members to support local businesses through organized "shop local" events.

Why: Building relationships with small businesses can lead to sponsorships, discounts for church members, and a stronger, more interconnected community.

By actively building and maintaining these relationships, churches can create a supportive network that enhances their ability to serve the community effectively.

DEVELOP THESE RELATIONSHIPS

Facilitating Resource Access

Example: A pastor with strong ties to local banks can more easily secure funding for community projects.

Why: Leaders with good relationships with key community entities can tap into resources that may otherwise be inaccessible, ensuring the church can support various programs and initiatives effectively.

Enhancing Outreach Efforts

Example: A youth leader who collaborates with local schools can coordinate after-school programs that benefit the church and the students.

Why: Effective outreach often requires collaboration. Leaders who build strong relationships can extend the church's reach, engaging more people and addressing broader community needs.

Building Credibility and Trust

Example: A church leader who actively engages with city officials can advocate for community concerns more effectively.

Why: When community entities know and respect church leaders, it enhances the church's credibility. This trust can lead to more fruitful collaborations and significant community influence.

Creating Synergy for Greater Impact

Example: Coordinating with local health centers to provide wellness programs during church events.

Why: Leaders who build bridges can create synergistic partnerships that multiply the impact of church initiatives, leading to more comprehensive and effective community service.

Promoting Unity and Shared Vision

Example: A senior pastor who networks with various community leaders can align church initiatives with broader community goals.

Why: Good relationships with community entities promote unity, shared purpose, cooperation, and a collective effort towards common goals.

Ensuring Sustainability

Example: A church administrator who maintains relationships with local businesses can secure ongoing sponsorships and support.

Why: Sustainable community service requires long-term support. Leaders who build and maintain relationships can ensure continuous resources and backing for church programs.

By actively nurturing these relationships, church leaders enhance the church's ability to serve its congregation and the broader community and build a network of support that can lead to a more significant and lasting impact. These relationships create a thriving, engaged, and unified community.

We would be remiss if we did not mention that we never, under any circumstance, compromised the Gospel of Jesus Christ in any way. "Do two walk together, unless they have agreed to meet?... For the Lord GOD does nothing without revealing his secret to his servants the prophets" (Amos 3:3,7).

If the destination or the route to the destination is hostile to the Cross and the contents of His Word, then we don't build the relationship. As is found in Amos, God will reveal his plans to His servants, but we must seek Him. Before establishing any relationship with any person or entity, please pray and seek the will of the Father.

NO YOUTH, NO CHURCH SOULUTIONS

10
CONTEND IN THE CULTURE

What is going on?

The following headlines, drawn from various news outlets across the country, highlight the alarming rise of violence among youth:

"Chicago Teen Charged in Fatal Stabbing During School Fight" – A teenager in Chicago was charged with the murder of a classmate after a violent altercation at school.

"Philadelphia Teen Charged in Deadly Stabbing Over Social Media Feud" – A teenager in Philadelphia faced charges for killing another youth during a confrontation sparked by a social media argument.

"Baltimore Teenager Found Guilty of Murder in Brutal Beating Case" – A teenager in Baltimore was convicted of murder after a violent attack that led to the death of another youth.

"San Francisco Teen Charged with Fatal Stabbing at a Party" – A San Francisco teenager was arrested for fatally stabbing another teen during a house party.

"Atlanta Teen Killed in Drive-By Shooting Related to School Rivalries" – A teenager in Atlanta was fatally shot in a drive-by incident linked to ongoing school rivalries.

"Miami Teen Arrested for Bullying-Related Suicide of Classmate" – A teenager in Miami was charged after severe bullying led to the suicide of a fellow student.

"Dallas Youth Charged in Deadly Knife Attack During School Lunch" – A teenager in Dallas was arrested for a fatal knife attack that occurred during lunchtime at school.

"Spartanburg Youth Arrested for Role in Brutal Beating Death of Classmate" – A teenager in Spartanburg was charged with involvement in the beating death of a fellow student.

"Greenville Teen Charged in School Shooting Incident That Injured Multiple Students" – A teenager in Greenville faced charges for a shooting at a high school that resulted in injuries to several students.

The last two headlines are from our city, just down the street from our home.

Martin Luther King Jr. said, "Darkness cannot drive out darkness; only light can do that. Hate cannot drive out hate; only love can do that."

This quote emphasizes the importance of practicing non-violence and compassion in adversity. It reminds us that our most potent weapon against hate and darkness is love and light. This world needs truth, and God's Word is light.

The headlines involving youth in violent incidents paint a stark and troubling picture of the challenges facing our communities. It's easy to feel overwhelmed or disheartened when confronted with such grim reports. The persistent issues of shootings, stabbings, and severe bullying among our youth might make us want to throw in the towel, feeling that the problems are insurmountable.

However, these headlines should ignite a fire to roll up our sleeves and work even harder. They underscore the urgent need for our involvement, not just as educators or leaders, but as compassionate individuals committed to supporting positive change.

These headlines reveal a dark cloud hanging over our youth, and it's crucial to recognize that the problem isn't just out there in the streets; it also lurks within our schools, children's churches, and youth groups. It's disheartening to realize that many of the students we see misbehaving or getting into trouble are in our youth groups.

This crisis is not just about physical violence but also about the deeper, often unspoken issues of emotional and psychological turmoil. It's a reminder that faith and positive values need to be more than just concepts we teach—they need to be experiences that resonate deeply with our young people. While faith comes by hearing, it's clear that hearing alone isn't enough. We must ensure that our teachings and interactions with youth are meaningful and impactful.

SO, WHAT CAN WE DO?

1. Focus on Emotional and Mental Well-being: Integrating lessons on emotional intelligence, resilience, and conflict resolution into our programs is essential. Equip our youth with the tools they need to handle their emotions and relationships in healthy ways.

2. Build Stronger Relationships: Develop genuine, supportive relationships with the youth in our care. Sometimes, just knowing that someone cares can make a huge difference in a young person's life.

3. Promote Positive Role Models: Highlight and celebrate positive role models who embody the values we want to instill. Show our youth that navigating life's challenges with integrity and grace is possible.

4. Address Root Causes: Look beyond the immediate behavior and address the underlying issues contributing to violence and misbehavior. Here, we sometimes notice that what we find might include family dynamics, community environments, or personal struggles.

5. Create Safe Zones: Ensure that our schools, churches, and youth groups are safe places where young people feel valued and heard. Being valued and heard can help prevent violence and encourage open communication.

6. Increase the Depth of Teaching: We must take teaching and mentoring seriously, move beyond superficial lessons, and engage with our youth on a deeper level. Address their real-life issues, concerns, and struggles with empathy and understanding. We have to speak the truth. Youth want to hear the truth.

Psalm 15:2 tells us to speak the truth from your heart. It's a misconception that speaking truth from the heart requires a gentle, soft tone or an apologetic posture to avoid offense. Perhaps it's not about tone but about content.

Truth is confrontational, and it's liberating. There's so much irreverent babble and false claims circulating on social media. Galatians 4:6 asks, "So have I become your enemy by telling you the truth?"

Truth is translated from "alétheia," meaning verity, fact, and certainty. Truth is God's purpose through Christ. 1 Timothy 6:20 says, "Oh Timothy, guard the deposit entrusted to you. Avoid the irreverent babble and contradictions of what is falsely called 'knowledge.'"

For there to be a contradiction, someone's position must be wrong.

We live in a time when lies are being presented as truth. We must train our students to detect babble. And yes, babble is wrong. That's why it's called babble—it is vague, without a solid position, meant to throw you off. Babble equals foolish, vain information. We must teach our students not to let empty words confuse them and to listen to strange sounds and philosophies. To recognize the strange, they must first know what sound doctrine is. Be free from the fear of sounding judgmental by declaring that something is WRONG or doesn't sound right. The older saints used to say, "Right is right, and wrong is wrong."

2 Corinthians 4:2 suggests that we reject all shameful deeds and underhanded methods. We don't try to trick anyone or distort the Word of God. We tell the truth before God, and all who are honest know this.

2 Corinthians 10:5 states, "Casting down imaginations, and every high thing that exalteth itself against the knowledge of God and bringing into captivity every thought to the obedience of Christ."

Another translation of that scripture reads, "We demolish arguments and every pretension that sets itself up against the knowledge of God, and we take captive every thought to make it obedient to Christ."

Once we understand that the Word of God is not subjective but objective, we can speak it boldly. Truth is not subjective. Objectivity lies outside of us.

Your students should know that by professing to be Christians, many will say negative things about their faith. Frank Turek says, "It's not your job to refute what they say. It's their job to support what they say."

Be encouraged to teach the truth from your heart. Truth from the heart is like water from a well or vegetables from a garden. Truth from your heart is not about the approach; it's about the place where truth should be hoarded. You can't speak the truth from your heart if no truth is stored away in your heart.

Psalm 119:11 says, "Your word I have hidden in my heart ('levav') that I might not sin against God."

The word "hide" comes from the Hebrew word "psafan," which means to hide by covering over, hoarding, reserving, keeping, protecting, lay-up continually, accumulating, esteem, and honor. Today, we, as youth leaders, pastors, and teachers, should teach our students how to become professional hoarders. In other words, we should teach them to become good at hoarding God's Word.

Have you ever seen a hoarder?

Well, let me tell you, hoarders are quite an interesting bunch! First, they tend to collect just about anything and everything, from old newspapers to empty plastic bags. They also have difficulty removing items, even if they are entirely useless. And finally, their homes often resemble a maze, with narrow pathways winding through piles and piles of clutter. It's like an episode of "Hoarders" come to life!

That's exactly how the Word of God should be in our hearts. When the enemy comes to us with his tricks, he is literally confronted with the Word of God in every inch of our hearts he is trying to contaminate. There is no place the enemy can go where he is not met with the Word of God. This sentiment, of course, is the testimony of a person doing a good job of hoarding God's Word in their heart. Psalm 1 says we are blessed when we meditate on God's Word, day and night.

In Genesis, darkness and disorder were upon the face of the earth. In Genesis, darkness and disorder were upon the face of the deep until God's Spirit corrected the chaos with order and confronted darkness with light.

In today's culture, darkness is also on the face of the deep. Social media is a chaotic place full of darkness. Why do I say it is full of darkness? Just scroll for 60 seconds and note how many immoral and negative images, videos, quotes, or music appear.

Social media has fundamentally changed the way we communicate.

Have you noticed a shift in basic social skills among our youth?

With students spending so much time on social media platforms, it often feels as though they are disconnected from the real world and real-life relationships.

Many of our students appear to be in a trance, heavily influenced by social media. This behavior is evident from a mile away. Social media addiction can harm mental health, with more and more students struggling with anxiety, depression, and a lack of productivity. We find ourselves asking, "What are you doing all day?"

Students are being exposed to things they should not be learning at an early age. The law of first truth is, unfortunately, causing them to align with false information and question the truth when it is presented.

You can tell when a kid has been bullied online. Their behavior changes, their anxiety levels are high, and their psychological state is noticeably different. They are not the same person—Jeremiah, for example, is not the same. Social media is a hotspot for bullying; your students don't even have to leave home to be bullied.

I believe parents should take control by monitoring their child's screen time. When screen time increases on social media, you may notice a change in your student's disposition.

Depression and lower self-esteem may start to surface. Social media is unrealistic, and our students must understand that these unrealistic expectations are illusions, often causing the negative feelings social media can bring.

Please be aware of the schemes of darkness that our students face so that you know what to teach, how to teach, and what to fast and pray for.

Every youth leader should be familiar with the social media platforms that youth frequent. If your students are on these platforms, they have likely been exposed to adult content, profanity, violence, and illegal activity—even as young as six or fifteen years old.

SOCIAL MEDIA

Facebook (FB)

Adult Content: Despite efforts to moderate, explicit adult content can still appear due to the sheer volume of user-generated posts. Users might encounter inappropriate material if it is not filtered correctly.

Profanity: Facebook has community standards against hate speech and profanity, but some content can slip through, particularly in comment sections and posts.

Violence: Posts or videos depicting violence can sometimes be found despite Facebook's measures to detect and remove such content. Exposure to graphic violence can still occur.

Instagram (IG) and Finsta

Adult Content: Instagram's visual nature can sometimes lead to sharing suggestive or adult content. The platform tries to regulate this but often relies on user reports.

Profanity: While Instagram has filters to limit profanity, users can still encounter explicit language, particularly in comments and user-generated content.

Violence: Violent content, including graphic images and videos, can appear, especially if shared through direct messages or stories.

TikTok

Adult Content: TikTok's algorithm can sometimes recommend content with sexual or suggestive themes despite efforts to moderate it.

Profanity: The platform's wide range of user-generated

content means explicit language is often present, especially in videos and comments.

Violence: Videos depicting violence, including pranks gone wrong or aggressive behavior, can sometimes appear on the platform.

Twitter

Adult Content: Twitter has fewer adult content restrictions than other platforms. Explicit content can often be encountered, even with user-applied filters.

Profanity: Twitter's open nature means profanity is common, especially in tweets and replies. While moderation exists, it is not always practical.

Violence: The platform has had issues with the spread of violent content and threats. Such content can still be present in tweets and replies even with monitoring.

YouTube (YT)

Adult Content: YouTube actively removes explicit content, but videos with suggestive themes or links to adult content can still be found, especially in user-generated content.

Profanity: While YouTube has policies against explicit language, some content creators may still use profanity, particularly in non-monetized or unfiltered videos.

Violence: Violent content or graphic imagery can occasionally be found despite YouTube's efforts to enforce community guidelines.

Twitch

Adult Content: Twitch's live streaming format can sometimes lead to the accidental or intentional display of adult content. While the platform employs moderators, some content can still slip through.

Profanity: Twitch streams often include profanity, especially in unsupervised or user-generated content. The platform has tools to manage this, but issues persist.

Violence: Violence can be depicted in some streams or games, and while Twitch has guidelines to manage this, certain content may still be broadcast.

General Social Media Challenges

"Tide Pod Challenge": Encourages the consumption of laundry detergent pods, leading to severe health risks.

"Cinnamon Challenge": Involves eating a spoonful of cinnamon without drinking water, which can cause respiratory issues and choking.

"Bird Box Challenge": Encourages users to perform tasks blindfolded, leading to dangerous situations and accidents.

"Kiki Challenge": Involves dancing outside of a moving car, which can result in injuries or fatalities.

"Blue Whale Challenge": A series of harmful tasks that culminate in self-harm or suicide.

DECODING TEXT MESSAGE EXAMPLES PARENTS NEED TO KNOW

"GN": Typically means "Good Night," but can sometimes imply a more flirtatious or inappropriate conversation.

"WTW": Means "What's the Word?" but can be used to initiate or discuss sensitive topics.

"HMU": Stands for "Hit Me Up," which could be used to arrange meetings that may not always be appropriate.

"BRB": "Be Right Back," often used to step away temporarily but can also signal a switch to another conversation or platform.

EMOJIS USED TO COMMUNICATE NEGATIVE MEANINGS:

Use the following descriptions to determine the emojis used to depict each statement.

1. Can be used to insult or demean someone by suggesting they are worthless or unpleasant.

2. Sometimes used to imply violence or threats in a figurative sense.

3. Can be used metaphorically to indicate a dangerous or explosive situation.

4. Used to express anger or hostility, sometimes in a confrontational or threatening manner.

5. This combination of emojis suggests "kiss slow."

6. Together, these emojis imply "you're going to be lucky tonight."

7. A playful phrase where "cake" is often used in slang to describe someone's body.

8. In certain contexts, this phrase suggests oral sex

9. These plant-related emojis are often used to represent marijuana, symbolizing cannabis culture or consumption.

10. This emoji represents prescription drugs like Percocet, a painkiller that is sometimes misused recreationally.

11. Similar to Percocet, Xanax is also represented by this emoji, indicating its use as an anti-anxiety medication, often discussed in both medical and recreational contexts.

12. Molly (MDMA), another drug, is often associated with party culture and euphoria.

Emoji Answers:

1. Pile of Poop

2. Knife

3. Bomb

4. Angry face with horns

5. Two kisses and a Turle (*the turtle represents a slow pace and the kiss emojis symbolizes affection or romantic gestures*)

6. Four-leaf Clover and Moon (*here, the four-leaf clover signifies good fortune and the moon refers to nighttime*)

7. Swimmer and a Slice of Cake (the swimming emoji refers to "swim," creating a flirtatious or humorous expression; while the slice of cake is used to describe someone's body (usually the backside)

8. Lollipop (*oral sex is often connected to the lollipop's association with sucking*)

9. Leaf or Leaves

10. Pill

11. Pill

12. Celebration emojis (i.e., with the Megaphone with Confetti)and a Stars or Sprinkles

FASHION AND ITS INFLUENCE

Evolution of Fashion: Fashion is increasingly a tool for self-expression and identity. What's considered stylish or acceptable can heavily influence behavior and self-perception. It's a question of *what* you have on and *why* you have it on.

Modesty and Trends: Modesty in fashion is often seen as outdated, with many current trends embracing more revealing or edgy styles. This shift reflects changing cultural values and influences. Unfortunately, what was once considered provocative is now viewed as conservative.

Influences: Social media and celebrities, particularly athletes and hip-hop artists, heavily influence fashion trends among students. These trends often encourage the imitation of styles that can be provocative or emphasize high-status symbols.

DANCES AND GESTURES

Middle Finger Gesture: Universally recognized as an offensive gesture, symbolizing disrespect or anger. It's commonly used in confrontations and can escalate tensions. Be aware that there are more gestures that convey this message, and you may not be familiar with them.

Other Gestures: Gestures such as the "OK" hand sign

can be misinterpreted or used inappropriately in some contexts. Some dance moves might also symbolize rebellion or aggression, often popularized by certain music genres or social media trends.

THE BIG PICTURE

All this negativity, doom, and gloom is just the tip of the iceberg and should guide us toward the content we should teach that will counter the culture. Students must grasp what we believe and why we believe it before we can teach them how to defend the faith, also known as apologetics. Apologetics is not reserved for seminary students or pastors.

In 2007, accodrding to the Pew Research Center 78% of the U.S. population, or 178 million people, identified as Christian. By 2014, that number declined to 71%, or 173 million.

As of the 2017 report, the percentage of the U.S. population identifying as Christian dropped to 63%. Between 2007 and 2017, in only 10 years, the US population identifying as Christian dropped 14%.

Table 4. Pew Research Center and the General Social Survey

Research suggests Christianity is not "sticky."

In other words, youth are raised Christian but do not remain Christian. Every parent and church must ask themselves, *WHY?* We submit that there are many eloquent and philosophical answers. Still, John 12:32 gives us a simple one: we are lifting everything, but Jesus and we haven't taught them apologetics. Sunday school and children's church are filled with teaching our kids "the story of" Noah, David and Goliath, and Jonah, but when do we transition them to doctrine, to the tenets of our faith—why do we believe what we believe? In other words, from milk to meat. Many adults haven't made this transition, so our youth are confused and uninterested. It's the blind leading the blind.

Ask your children. They are being taught evolution as if it is fact, the Big Bang Theory as if the "science is settled," and that gender is fluid with more than two sexes—all of this in elementary school. The church's silence is deafening.

As parents, youth leaders, aunts, and uncles, we are obligated to equip our kids. No offense to any pastors reading this, but we are failing our young people. The church is supposed to be the training center for the saints so we can be equipped with the TRUTH and compel others to come.

Sermons about my house and car is on the way are played out while our youth have fundamental questions about the faith. If you have unanswered questions about the beginning, everything else in the Bible becomes questionable.

WHAT IS APOLOGETICS?

Apologetics is the discipline of defending a position (often religious) through the systematic use of information. Jude calls it, "contending for the faith."

If I could sum up this year and the last ten, it's the era of "do what you want."

Or, as a popular atheist coined, "Do what thou wilt shall

be the whole of the law."

But Jesus said to deny yourself, take up your cross, and follow HIM!

What does God say about religion?

James 1:27 states, "Pure and undefiled religion before God and the Father is this: to visit orphans and widows in their trouble and to keep oneself unspotted from the world."

He made a point to say, "pure and undefiled."

Why?

He knew many heresies were active and on the way.

As we explore the doubts that arise from unanswered questions, it's important to address certain heresies and ideas that contradict Biblical doctrine.

At first glance, you might find these 'isms' intimidating, but once you look beyond the terminology, you'll see how they are woven into everyday life and media. Even Christians must be vigilant not to embrace these fallacies when they encounter them. By equipping our students with knowledge about false doctrines early on, we can help them become solid Christians, grounded in their faith.

Pelagianism: The belief, attributed to the British monk Pelagius, that human beings can earn salvation by their efforts—Ephesians 2:8-9: "For by grace are ye saved through faith; and that not of yourselves: it is the gift of God: Not of works, lest any man should boast."

Docetism: First mentioned in a letter by Bishop Serapion of Antioch, it is the belief that Jesus only seemed to be human and that his human form was an illusion—John 1:14: "And the Word became flesh and dwelt among us, and we beheld His glory, the glory as of the only begotten of the Father, full of grace and truth."

Adoptionism: A non-trinitarian theological teaching that Jesus was adopted as God's Son at either his baptism, resurrection, or ascension—Matthew and Luke present Jesus as the Son of God. John 1:1: "In the beginning was the Word, and the Word was with God, and the Word was God." Don't confuse the spirit of adoption mentioned in Romans 8:15 with Adoptionism. We move from children of wrath, according to Ephesians 5:2, to children of God. "Abba" is a term of endearment Jewish children call their father, adopted or natural. Paul is saying we are no longer servants; we are children, as if we were part of the original chosen.

Marcionism: A belief attributed to Marcion of Sinope (Rome) that the "wrathful" Hebrew God was a separate and lower entity than the all-forgiving God of the New Testament. But Peter said in Acts 3:13: "The God of Abraham, Isaac, and Jacob, the God of our fathers, glorified His Servant Jesus, whom you delivered up and denied in the presence of Pilate when he was determined to let Him go."

Matthew 5:17: "Do not think that I came to destroy the Law or the Prophets. I did not come to destroy but to fulfill."

Gnosticism: Perhaps the most dangerous heresy that threatened the early church during the first three centuries, Gnosticism is influenced by philosophers like Plato. It is based on two false premises: dualism regarding spirit and matter (asserting that matter is inherently evil and spirit is good) and the belief that anything done in the body, even the grossest sin, has no meaning because real life exists only in the spirit realm. Gnostics claim to possess an elevated knowledge, a "higher truth" or "gnosis" known only to a select few—Mysticism. Christianity asserts that there is one source of Truth, and that is the Bible, the inspired, inerrant Word of the living God, is the only infallible rule of faith and practice (John 17:17; 2 Timothy 3:15-17; Hebrews 4:12).

Gnosticism has shown up in black culture. It's all-over hip-hop music. Many artists leads love the gnostics. Listen to the lyrics: "dropping science" and "ciphers"; these reference Gnosticism.

The 5 Percent Nation of gods and earths, and now the Hebrew Israelites, is also Gnosticism—salvation by knowledge. The black man is god, and the black woman is earth. Fifteen percent know the truth (gnosis), 10% keep the world in the dark, and they are the 5% whose calling is to enlighten the world.

"For we wrestle not against flesh and blood, but against principalities, against powers, against the rulers of the darkness of this world, against spiritual wickedness in high places" (Ephesians 6:12).

The enemy does not want youth to know how to interpret the Bible. He wants them clueless, ignorant, and unlearned so he can keep them bound. The acronym BIBLE stands for "Basic Instructions Before Leaving Earth."

Think about it—no Bible, no instructions. What topic is more important than properly interpreting the Bible?

Imagine thinking a yield sign is a green light all your life. You will likely start to trace who told you or didn't teach you how to properly read a yield sign before getting your license. Promoting responsible Bible interpretation also highlights that there is an irresponsible way. A proper way highlights that there is an improper way. If there's a system for interpreting the Bible, there can easily be a fluid way that yields a particular understanding. Rightly dividing the Word of Truth highlights that there is a wrong way to divide the Word of Truth.

Jesus used parables to encourage us to look twice and dig deeper. There's a reward for those who diligently seek understanding. When reading scripture with students, consider avoiding the question, "What does this scripture mean to you?"

Instead, focus on articulating what stands out to you in this passage.

This will help them understand that there is only one meaning—one truth. This is important to emphasize in a "My Truth" generation.

To be clear, there is only one core meaning, though it can be applied in many ways.

For example, traffic signs have one specific meaning. If you were to break a traffic law and argue in court that the sign meant something different to you, it wouldn't hold up. The DMV suggests that if you find yourself puzzled by interpreting traffic signs, it's studying and understanding them properly is best.

This concept aligns with 2 Timothy 2:15: "Study to show thyself approved unto God, a workman that needeth not to be ashamed, rightly dividing the word of truth." The term "study" in Greek is "spoudazo," meaning to hasten, make haste, give diligence, labor, and exert effort. "Dividing" in Greek is "orthotomeo," referring to cutting straight, teaching the truth directly and correctly, and maintaining a straight course.

Yes, it takes work, as you can see, but in this context, let's use an acronym for WORK:

W–Will. Skill starts with will. Careful Biblical interpretation is a choice. We should seek to draw near, respect the process, and be committed. Are you willing to dig for wisdom?

O—Observation. What does the text say? When you break the speed limit when reading the text it will lead to misinterpretation. Pay careful attention and consider being systematic in your observation. Author and Bible teacher, Howard Hendrick, champions observation of the text.

R—Re-read and Research. We know in carpentry it is common to practice to measure twice, cut once. Let's encourage students to trade casual reading for intentional reading. Focus on *What, How, Who, When, and Where* it is being said?

K—Keys. These are some tools to help you as you gear up to teach your students how to interpret the Bible. These tools can be passed on to your students as well. Tecarta app, Bible Project, Translations, Counsel, English Grammar Manual, and Bibletools.org. Many of these resources have concordances and commentaries. A concordance is a reference tool that lists every word in a text and their occurrences, helping readers analyze language, themes, and context. You could explain to a kid that a concordance is like a giant word finder that helps you see where every word in a book appears so you can understand what the book is talking about.

As stated in the creativity chapter, being creative is key to making Bible study engaging for youth. Fun approaches include interactive games, storytelling, and creative arts, all while integrating accurate historical and cultural contexts. Using tech tools, music, and group discussions can enhance their understanding and make learning enjoyable.

IF IT WERE MY YOUTH GROUP

I would do a series in Genesis if it were my youth group. Genesis is one of my favorite books. I've heard it said that if you doubt Genesis, you will not reach Revelation. I like to put it this way.

Genesis before Golgotha or Creation before the Cross. A popular Christian apologist says that Genesis records the greatest miracle, Genesis 1. Think about it: why would I believe God raised Jesus from the dead if I am having doubts that a God is powerful enough to create something out of nothing?

I also appreciate an organization that helps teachers, parents, and students through Genesis.

The organization "Answers in Genesis" is great for helping youth be firm in their faith because it provides Biblically based answers to questions about science, history, and culture from a creationist perspective. The site offers engaging resources like articles, videos, and interactive content that help students understand and defend their beliefs while addressing common challenges to faith. This approach strengthens their understanding and confidence in their faith by integrating scientific and historical evidence with biblical teachings.

Think about it. Genesis covers identity, gender roles, morality, purpose, God as creator, science, worship, and more. Genesis is stacked! Myles Munroe said, "If you don't know the purpose of something, abuse is inevitable."

Teaching youth about their God-given purpose and position will help them live lives that align with God's will. The purpose is like guardrails. Do we see students seemingly acting like they don't have any restraints? Yes, of course. A lack of understanding of their purpose is one of the main reasons. If that's the case, this issue should intentionally trigger a teaching or curriculum.

YOUTH VIOLENCE

Given the increased incidents of youth violence in our city, I would implement a teaching series called "Peace Makers: Building a Culture of Non-Violence." We would draw from Genesis to understand God's call for peace and harmony.

Scriptural Basis:

Genesis 4:6-7: "Then the LORD said to Cain, 'Why are you angry? Why is your face downcast? If you do what is right, will you not be accepted? But if you do not do what is right, sin is crouching at your door; it desires to have you, but you must rule over it.'"

This passage helps address anger and the importance of controlling our responses.

Activities would include:

1. **Role-Playing Scenarios:** Practicing peaceful conflict resolution techniques.

2. **Group Discussions:** Exploring how to manage anger and resolve conflicts biblically.

3. **Guest Speakers:** Learning from community leaders

who work with at-risk youth.

DRUG ABUSE

If it were my youth group, to address the rising issue of drug abuse among teens, I would start a series called "Freedom in Christ: Overcoming Addiction and Finding True Freedom," using Genesis to illustrate the importance of making godly choices and avoiding destructive behaviors.

Scriptural Basis

Genesis 39:9: "No one is greater in this house than I am. My master has withheld nothing from me except you because you are his wife. How then could I do such a wicked thing and sin against God?" This passage, where Joseph refuses Potiphar's wife, highlights the importance of resisting temptation and remaining faithful to God.

Activities would include:

1. **Support Groups:** Providing a place for discussing struggles and offering support.
2. **Educational Workshops:** Partnering with local organizations for drug abuse education. **Testimonies:** Sharing stories of overcoming challenges through faith.

BULLYING

In response to high rates of bullying, I would implement a series called "Unconditional Love: Responding to Bullying with Christ's Compassion," drawing from Genesis to understand God's view of human dignity and kindness.

Scriptural Basis

Genesis 1:27: "So God created mankind in his own image, in the image of God he created them; male and female he created them." This passage emphasizes the inherent value of every individual, which can help counteract bullying and promote respect and compassion.

Activities would include:

1. **Empathy Exercises:** Activities to understand and empathize with others' feelings.

2. **Anti-Bullying Campaigns:** Organizing campaigns that promote kindness and respect.

3. **Peer Mentoring:** Pairing older students with younger ones to create a supportive environment.

SELF-ESTEEM ISSUES

To tackle low self-esteem and body image issues, I would start a series called "Expensive": Embracing Your True Worth," using Genesis to affirm each person's worth and purpose in God's creation.

Scriptural Basis:

Genesis 1:31: "God saw all that he had made, and it was very good." This passage reassures that God's creation, including everyone, is valuable and worthy.

Activities would include:

1. **Affirmation Exercises:** Write and share positive affirmations based on Scripture.

2. **Self-Worth Workshops:** Discuss identity and value as

created by God.

3. **Art Therapy:** Use creative expression to celebrate your identity in Christ and tie in Psalm 139:14.

Youth leaders, while you are not the parents of the students you lead, understanding these aspects can help you communicate with parents and guardians about the complexities of social media, fashion, and cultural trends affecting their children. Parents are busy and may only sometimes have time to pay attention during their day-to-day survival. However, monitoring and guiding students regarding these influences can significantly impact their well-being and development. We are standing in the gap. We must support parents and students contend in the culture.

NO YOUTH, NO CHURCH SOULUTIONS

CONCLUSION

As we reach the end of this journey through "No Youth No Church SOULutions: The Missing Pieces to Build a Thriving Youth Ministry," we want you to envision a future where every youth ministry—whether in a small church or a large congregation—flourishes with energy and impact. Imagine a community where every young person feels valued, heard, and equipped to lead with faith and confidence.

Our mission has been clear: to identify and address the missing pieces that, once tackled, will transform our ministries into powerful forces of hope and transformation. These SOULutions are not just strategies; they are the keys to a future where our churches are vibrant and dynamic, driven by the passion and potential of our youth.

Bottom Line: Embrace these SOULutions with dedication and vision. The future of your youth ministry and church can be radiant and full of possibility. By addressing these missing pieces, you are building a ministry and creating a lasting legacy of faith and vitality.

Your church won't just survive; it will thrive, fueling the growth of disciples, passing the torch of faith, and witnessing salvation and healing through your efforts. Let's turn this vision into reality and watch our youth lead us into a new era of transformation and grace.

ACKNOWLEDGMENTS

To Our Publisher

We extend our deepest gratitude to our publisher for believing in our vision and bringing this book to life. Your support and expertise have been invaluable throughout this journey.

To Our Parents

Our heartfelt thanks go to our parents, whose love and support have been the foundation of our lives. You are our number one supporters, and we deeply appreciate everything you have done for us. Your encouragement to dream big, maintain a healthy marriage, and grow in faith has been game-changing.

To Those Who Have Inspired Us

We are grateful to all who have inspired us to be better Christians and to honor others. Your influence has guided us in our pursuit to please our Lord and Savior, Jesus Christ, and to hear God say, "Well done."

We are also passionate about preparing the next generation to contend for the faith, and we owe much of this passion to the great apologists defending the truth with courage.

To Our Loved Ones

We honor our siblings and friends, who are precious to us. Your support has been a treasured part of our lives, and we want to acknowledge you for your integral role in our journey.

To Churches, Schools, and Organizations

To every church, school, and organization that has invited or will invite us: Thank you for trusting us with your time and allowing us to share our passion. We are committed to speaking with excellence and sincerity.

MEET
AL & LEX

In a world where the digital and artistic realms intersect, the unique talents of Alphaeus and Alexias Anderson come to the forefront. Known as "Alph and Lex" in their YouTube community, they embody the harmony of security and innovation.

Meet Cyber Security VP Alexias Anderson, a virtuoso in the realm of cyber defense and the music business. With a diverse set of skills that spans beyond the boundaries of technology and artistry, Alexias is the proud wife of Alphaeus and enjoys traveling the world with him. As a Music Supervisor from Berklee College, Alexias orchestrates melodies and safeguards intellectual property. Naturally a strategic thinker, Alexias enhanced her skills by adding an MBA and other certifications to her degree in Management Information Systems, making her an asset in any situation requiring her professional expertise.

Driven to empower the next generation, Alphaeus founded one of the largest Youth Gospel Choir in Gospel and later established the Pure N Heart Foundation with Alexias, where the melodies of hope and the tech world harmonize. Though Alphaeus is a triple threat, a musician, producer, and songwriter, accoladed with two (2) Stellar Awards and a Dove Nomination, melodies of success don't stop there. He also has a degree in Christian Ministries, with a minor in Music.

Alphaeus believes in sharing the truth through an apologetics approach. He has written a book titled "Youth Magnet: 5 Elements to Empower and Attract Youth to Your Church." Amidst these accomplishments, Alphaeus finds time to educate as an Adjunct Professor at USC Upstate, nurturing minds and hearts through Gospel Music. Like Alexias, he looks forward to packing his bags and traveling the world with his wife.

As Alphaeus and Alexias continue to weave together the threads of technology, music, ministry, education, and artistry, they compose a symphony of security with a global reach. They hope to leave a lasting legacy through philanthropic work, courses, and content.

www.ingramcontent.com/pod-product-compliance
Lightning Source LLC
Chambersburg PA
CBHW051546010526
44118CB00022B/2602